FOUR SHORT BLASTS

The Gale of 1898 and
The Loss of the
Steamer Portland

FOUR SHORT BLASTS

The Gale of 1898 and
The Loss of the
Steamer Portland

PETER DOW BACHELDER

MASON PHILIP SMITH

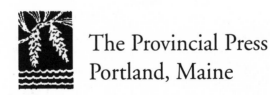

The Provincial Press
Portland, Maine

Copyright © 1998 Peter Dow Bachelder & Mason Philip Smith

SECOND (Humarock) EDITION

THE PROVINCIAL PRESS
98 Chestnut Street Suite 98W
P.O. Box 1020
Portland, ME 04104-1020

Portland *Battles The Gale*, the front cover painting, was painted by Roland Borduas of Portland, Maine, and is from the Collection of The Provincial Press. The colorful Boston Job Print lithograph and *Portland Advertiser* newspaper on the back cover courtesy of Kenneth E. Thompson Jr. *Last Trip To Boston*, the title-page illustration, is an original watercolor by Art Hahn from the Collection of The Provincial Press.

ISBN 0-931675-06-5
                    Library of Congress Cataloging—in—Publication Data
Bachelder, Peter Dow.
       Four short blasts the gale of 1898 and the loss of the steamer
       Portland / Peter Dow Bachelder, Mason Philip Smith.
              p.   cm.
       Includes bibliographical references (p.   ) and index.
       ISBN 0—931675—06—5 (alk. paper)
       1. Windstorms——New England——History——19th century. 2. New England——History——19th century. 3. Ship-
       wrecks——New England——History——19th century. 4. Portland (Steamer) 5. Portland (Me.)—
       —History——19th century. 6. Eighteen ninety—eight, A.D. I. Smith,
        Mason Philip, 1933—   II. Title.
       F9.B137 1998
       974' .041-—dc21   98-34545
                                                                                      CIP

Dedicated To The Memory of

Jes Jessen Schmidt
Jessine Schmidt
Jorgen Jessen Schmidt
Anton Schmidt

Lost on the Steamer Portland
November 27, 1898

Books By Peter Dow Bachelder
The Lighthouses & Lightships of Casco Bay
Shipwrecks &Maritime Disasters of the Maine Coast
Museums & Historic Homes of Maine

Books by Mason Philip Smith
Confederates Downeast
Toward Arkhangelsk
Cycling Around Four Provinces
In The Netherlands (editor)

CONTENTS

Four Short Blasts has been more than two decades in the making. It was a project each of us talked and speculated about on countless occasions, as our research into the *Portland* gale brought us a deeper understanding of, and closer feeling for, this extraordinary weather event. But it was also one we never carried beyond the idea stage until last year.

One of us grew up with the *Portland* saga in his blood, as his great-aunt and great-uncle and their two children were lost when the *Portland* foundered and went to the bottom of the Atlantic Ocean.

As anyone who has ever attempted an undertaking of this sort knows, it can never happen without considerable cooperation and assistance from a wide assortment of sources. We owe a deep debt of gratitude to a host of wonderful people, who—occasionally on short notice—opened their homes, offices, or research facilities; searched their collections; and willingly shared their findings with us.

The memory of the late author and lecturer Edward Rowe Snow, who delved into the *Portland* gale at length, loomed large over our efforts, especially when we pored over his own storm-related collection in the Snow archives at Boston University.

As young men we both either attended his popular radio show, or walked the historic streets of Boston with him or plunged with him into his fantastic collection of martitime objects, maps, books, and ephemera at his Marshfield, Massachusetts, home.

We spent many enjoyable moments with Ed over the years, although perhaps none so poignant as the ones during a meal we shared following a late 1960s waterfront memorial service for the *Portland* victims.

Captain Joseph Roderick of North Truro relived fond memories of his nearly 40 years fishing the waters of Massachusetts Bay and described his 1950s experience of hauling aboard his vessel the remains of what may well be significant *Portland* wreckage.

Bob Greene, of Brooklyn, New York, graciously shared with us his knowledge of the family of Eben Heuston, second steward aboard *Portland*, and offered several other helpful details regarding the black members of the steamer's crew. Bob's contributions notably enriched the story.

Robert T. Mortimer of Falmouth, Maine, made his entire *Portland* collection available to us and allowed us to photograp, and include in this volume, several of his rare images.

We owe special thanks to history enthusiast Kenneth E. Thompson Jr. of Portland, who voluntarily passed along his own research into the *Portland* Gale, as well as images and mementos he has gathered over the years. The reminiscences of his great grandfather, Captain William D. Scott, who met the steamer *Portland* off Cape Ann the night of its fateful voyage, were particularly meaningful.

Chris Church, of *Show & Tell & Son*, Portland, provided invaluable help during several phases of our work, including information acquisition and image processing.

Acclaimed TV newsman/historian William P. Quinn of Orleans, Massachusetts, was a unique and invaluable source. From his incomparable collection of shipwreck photos and maritime lore, he cordially provided a broad range of noteworthy storm-related images, together with a host of other meaningful material. His prompt and willing cooperation in assisting our efforts meant a great deal to us, and the breadth and scope of the material he furnished has unquestionably enhanced the end result.

Historian William B. Jordan, Jr., of Portland, Maine, the acknowledged expert on Greater Portland history, shared with us the recollections of his grandmother who had journeyed through a storm aboard the *Portland* two weeks before the vessel's final trip from Boston to Portland. In addition Jordan assisted us as we searched Greater Portland cemeteries looking for the burial sites of those lost on the *Portland* and whose remains had been recovered.

We deeply appreciate, as well, the countless efforts of the many understanding and helpful people at the following institutions: Nicholas Noyes, Stephanie Philbrick and William Barry, Maine Historical Society; Nathan Lipfert, Director, and Robert Webb, Curator, Maine Maritime Museum; Frank Wihbey, Government Documents Librarian, Fogler Library, University of Maine at Orono; Dr. Howard B. Gotlieb, Director, and Charlie Niles, Research Assistant, Department of Special Collections, Mugar Library, Boston University; Jeffory Morris, Curator of Collections, and Lauren Guadazno, Visitor Services Manager, Pilgrim Monument & Provincetown Museum; Bruce T. Tarvers, President, Truro Historical Society, who was kind enough to open the society's museum during the off season; Debbie DeJonkers Berry, Provincetown Public Library; George Young and James Owens, National Archives & Records Administration, Waltham, MA; Paul F. Johnson, Curator of Maritime History, Smithsonian Institution, Washington, D.C. Likewise, the librarians and staff at: Portland Public Library, Portland, Maine; Ellsworth Public Library, Ellsworth, Maine; Maine State Library, Augusta, Maine; Hawthorne Library, Bowdoin College, Brunswick, Maine; and University of Southern Maine Library, Portland, Maine.

We also owe large debts of gratitude to our wives, Katherine J. Bachelder and Barbara Darrah Smith who showed great understanding of the time commitment required to research and complete this book. We are also indebted to: Howard Reiche, Falmouth, Maine; Leo Chabot, North Andover, Massachusetts; Harris G. Smith, Ipswich, Massachusetts; Ralph Lewis, Bath, Maine; Ron McCann, Portland, Maine; Dan Rodrigue, Dresden, Maine; Charles Burden, Brunswick, Maine; Arnold H. Valcour, Portland, Maine; William B. Jordan, Jr., Portland, Maine; C. J. Stevens, Phillips, Maine and James Elliott, Standish, Maine.

Peter Dow Bachelder   Mason Philip Smith
Ellsworth, Maine   Cape Elizabeth, Maine

June 25, 1998

New England's Weather: Its Origins and Influences

Air masses affecting New England's weather originate hundreds, often even thousands of miles away. Some are born in marine environments such as the stormy North Pacific Ocean and the ever-warm Gulf of Mexico; others develop in continental climes, including the cold reaches of northern Canada and the Arctic, the blazing deserts of the southwestern U.S. and northern Mexico. En route to the northeast they are typically modified to some extent, either by interacting with contrasting air masses or by the terrain over which they pass.

These weather systems are propelled by powerful steering currents several miles up in the atmosphere. Where the flow is strongest, weathercasters refer to the core as the *jet stream*—a powerful ribbon of air that typically speeds along at well over one hundred knots.

When the jet stream moves in an essentially west-to-east fashion, the resulting movement of systems is called *zonal* and is mostly storm-free. In a zonal flow, contrasting air masses—necessary to create stormy conditions—are kept apart. Colder, drier air is contained to the north, and warmer, moister air is prevented from flowing north. But when the jet develops undulations—a southerly dip is called a *trough*; a northerly bent, a *ridge*—warm and cold air frequently reach well beyond their normal ranges. Then, contrasting systems clash and the general weather pattern takes on more turbulent characteristics.

New England's more vigorous weather is frequently triggered when tropical air surges northward from the Gulf of Mexico or is drawn in from the Gulf Stream, a warm ocean current off the Atlantic seaboard. As these moisture-laden streams override outbreaks of dry, polar air spilling down from northern and east-central Canada, storminess is the inevitable result.

Storm Tracks and the Northeast

The northeastern U.S. has the dubious distinction of being a favorite area for differing air masses to do battle. Sometimes, an area of low pressure riding across the western U.S. will descend a trough in the mid-section of the country and tap Gulf moisture that sustains and strengthens it as it recurves toward the east coast. On other occasions, a low reaches a position near the Great Lakes, where it transfers energy to a secondary development off the mid-Atlantic states. In the latter case, the newly formed system—if the critical conditions come together at the right moment—will wind itself into a powerful ocean storm. When this happens, winds near the center of circulation sometimes reach hurricane force and, depending on the time of year and the amount of cold air north and west of the storm track, precipitation wrapping around the system falls as drenching rains or blinding snows.

America's Weather Pioneers

Mark Twain usually gets the credit for coining the phrase, "Everybody talks about the weather, but nobody ever does anything about it." Actually, it was his associate, Charles Dudley Warner, who penned the expression as part of an 1897 *Hartford Courant* editorial. Long before then, however, many Americans had shown a keen interest in trying to understand the atmosphere and what makes it tick, even if they couldn't influence it.

In the late eighteenth and early nineteenth centuries, John Jeffries, John Winthrop, and William Plumer were among the country's more prominent "weather scientists." Jeffries compiled two sets of detailed weather notes in Boston between 1774 and 1816 and was aboard the first scientific balloon ascent to measure the characteristics of free air from aloft. Winthrop and Plumer kept extensive diaries and journals at various locations around New England and in Washington, D.C.

Even such luminaries as Benjamin Franklin, George Washington, and Thomas Jefferson were significant contributors to the developing body of early weather knowledge. Franklin's experiments with lightning are well known, although few realize it was he who first recognized how storm systems move—a significant step in forecasting. Jefferson studied the nation's climate at length, routinely taking observations of temperature, atmospheric pressure, wind speed and direction, and sky conditions. George Washington faithfully kept a weather diary until the week he died.

Weather Forecasting Comes of Age

Soon after the founding fathers created a federal government, the study of weather became a part of the country's ongoing business. In 1814, the first American weather observer network was established within the U.S. Army's Medical Department. In 1870, Congress authorized a national weather service, as a branch of the Army Signal Service, and organized a network of reporting stations. Twenty-one years later, it created the U.S. Weather Bureau, which took over and expanded the duties of the Signal Corps.

Even with all this attention and activity, the science of meteorology was still in its relative infancy in the late nineteenth century. Forecasters had developed a basic understanding of how high and low pressure areas interact, but were largely limited to studying them in two dimensions. They knew little of what went on above the earth's surface, where the steering currents that move weather systems are located.

Prior to 1900, Weather Bureau headquarters in Washington gathered the latest conditions and issued forecasts twice a day, via electric telegraph, to each of its regional offices and branches. It also put out special statements, warnings, and advisories whenever threatening conditions warranted. The local offices, in turn, relayed the individual predictions and directives to neighboring subscribers such as railroads, steamship lines, and a host of commercial interests whose businesses served the public welfare.

Until the advent of wireless communication, daily newspapers brought the latest local weather news into America's homes. Most printed it on the front page of each edition. The popular byline included the current forecast and the next day's outlook, as well as brief statistics about the previous day's happenings, such as high and low temperatures and the amount of rain or snow that had fallen. Often, a paper captioned the forecast with an appropriate, single-descriptive word, ornamented by a cartoon image. One illustration showed a small child in Santa-style cap and mittens, holding a placard with the word *Snow* boldly displayed, while large flakes danced in the background.

Forecasting the Great Gale of November 26-27, 1898

The great gale of November 26-27, 1898, affected New England on Thanksgiving weekend—late Saturday through much of Sunday. While Weather Bureau prognosticators had no advance inkling of the storm's ultimate intensity and duration, nor a real sense of when it would affect the northeast, they did gauge its formation and movement with a fair amount of accuracy. On Friday evening, November 25, it was the timing of the forecast which left something to be desired:

> Forecast for Saturday: For New England, fair, continued cold, brisk westerly, shifting to southerly winds. For eastern New York, increasing cloudiness and rain or snow by Saturday night, rising temperature, winds shifting to brisk southerly.
> Outlook for Sunday: The weather in New England Sunday will be unsettled, and rain or snow is possible, most likely in the afternoon or night. The foul weather depends on the movement and development of a storm now apparently in the gulf of Mexico. The temperature will not change decidedly.

Saturday morning's early prediction was similar, but in light of rapidly changing conditions, Washington forecasters perceived a dramatic weather event in the making. Prior to noon, they issued special wind and snow advisories for "maritime, commercial, and traffic interests" and amended the previous advisory for the general public:

> Forecast for Maine, New Hampshire, and Vermont, heavy snow and warmer tonight; Sunday, snow and much colder; southeasterly winds shifting by tonight to northeasterly gales.
> For Massachusetts, Rhode Island, and Connecticut, heavy snow tonight; Sunday, snow, followed by clearing and much colder weather; southeasterly, shifting to northeasterly gales tonight, and northwesterly gales by Sunday.

A Storm for the Ages

The Saturday forenoon prognosis would prove all too true. What it did not—indeed, could not—take into account were the extreme conditions and accompanying destructiveness the approaching storm would unleash. The great gale of November 1898 would prove to be one for the record books—and one most New Englanders would not soon forget.

The steamer *Portland*.

Anatomy of the Great Gale

November weather over the northeastern United States during 1898 was about as close to ordinary as it ever gets—at least until the final few days of the month. Temperatures and rainfall amounts ranged close to normal, and the occasional snows that fell were mostly limited to the higher elevations of northern New England. This benign pattern would change abruptly over the Thanksgiving weekend, ushering in an unsettled period that would dominate the region over the next several weeks.

Before the month was out, the northeast coast—and southern New England, in particular—would suffer one of the greatest autumn storms of the nineteenth century. In some respects, it would compare with the most severe, regardless of the season. What would come to be called the Great Gale of November 1898, or simply the *Portland* Gale, would dump near-record snows in central Connecticut and Massachusetts, whip up hurricane force winds off Cape Cod, and push a devastating tidal surge across low-lying coastal areas from Long Island Sound to eastern Maine.

The resulting damage would be inestimable. In addition to the natural disaster—thousands of uprooted or broken trees and a major reconfiguration of coastal beaches, dunes, and waterways—tens of millions of dollars in structural damage would occur to homes, businesses, and properties. In today's dollars, the losses would be counted well into the billions.

But the greatest tragedies of all would be the several hundred lives lost, mostly in the scores of marine disasters that disrupted coastal commerce for days, even weeks afterward. At the forefront of these tragedies was the shocking loss of the passenger steamship *Portland*, in which more than 190 passengers and crew sailed to their doom as the storm raged around them.

Thanksgiving Day 1898 fell on November 24th, and the holiday weather across much of the eastern half of the U.S. was relatively quiet, if not downright serene. A bubble of high pressure over the Ohio valley was sending brisk northwest winds and slightly chillier than normal temperatures into New England and the northeast, behind a departing batch of showers. Further west, a weak low near Minnesota was shaking out a few, relatively unimportant snow flurries over the western Great Lakes, while a second low, taking shape over the western Gulf of Mexico, had begun pumping warm, moist air and accompanying raininess into portions of southern Louisiana and Mississippi.

By evening the high had retreated eastward as the Great Lakes low, now over Lake Superior, showed signs of slight strengthening. In its wake, the system's counter-clockwise rotation was bringing down a blast of cold, Arctic air from central Canada, sending temperatures in the northern Plains plummeting. Meanwhile, the southern low had tracked across the central Gulf and spread a mantle of cloudiness and scattered showers as far east as central Georgia.

Saturday morning, November 26, the weakening high was being squeezed off the New England coast. The Great Lakes low, sliding to the southeast, was now centered over eastern lower Michigan. The remaining energy from the patch of Gulf moisture was reorganizing at a point just off the southeast coast and had begun sending a steady rain into Charleston, South Carolina. Forecasters from the U.S. Weather Bureau's central office in Washington noted the two systems were connected by a trough—an elongated area of low air pressure which facilitates the transfer of one storm's energy to another. It was a condition they recognized as being a significant "weather maker." Professor E.B. Garriott, in charge of the forecast division of the Weather Bureau at the time, asserted a few weeks later:

> A distinctive feature of these storms is found in the fact that a development of destructive strength begins with a union at some point off the middle Atlantic or south New England coasts of two storms, one from the west or northwest, and the other from the south Atlantic coast.

And, indeed, conditions in the east began to change significantly through the daylight hours of Saturday, November 26. During the morning, the Michigan low advanced to near Pittsburgh, and the coastal depression, approach-

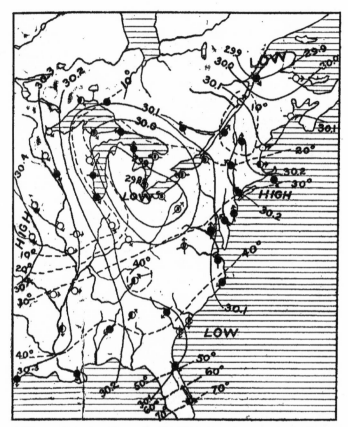

8:00 a.m., Saturday, November 26, 1898. Saturday morning's pleasant weather in New England gave little indication of what was soon to follow. Departing high pressure just south of Cape Cod was giving way to a trough of low pressure with centers over Toledo, Ohio, and off the Georgia coast. The result would bring intense storminess into the region within 12 hours.

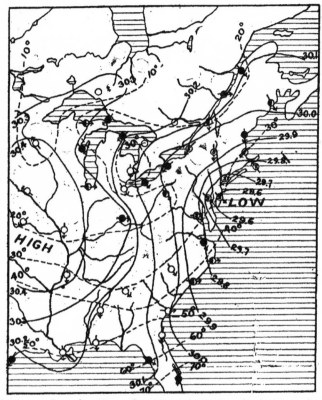

8:00 p.m., Saturday, November 26, 1898. During the day Saturday, the Midwest and Southeast lows merged into a single, rapidly deepening system off the mid-Atlantic coast. By eight p.m., the storm was centered near Atlantic City, New Jersey, and was causing a wide swath of snow across the northeastern states, from Washington to Boston.

ing Cape Hatteras, had started churning its way northeastward, slowly gaining strength and speed. Anticipating further development of the Hatteras system, forecasters at 10:30 a.m. ordered storm signals raised from Norfolk, Virginia, to Eastport, Maine. Within the warning area, southeast storm signals were decreed for the exposed sections of the New Jersey, New York, and Connecticut shores, and northeast signals for the entire New England coast—from Newport, Rhode Island, to Eastport. The warnings were accompanied by the following marine advisory:

> Storm central near Detroit moving east. East to northeast gales with heavy snow tonight. Wind will shift to west and northwest with much colder Sunday.

In addition, the following special snowfall advisory went out to all Weather Bureau offices in New York and New England, for immediate redistribution within each district:

> Heavy snow indicated for New York and New England tonight. Notify railroad and transportation interests.

By three o'clock Saturday afternoon, the coastal low—now spinning off Norfolk—had virtually absorbed the Midwest system into its circulation and was continuing to gather force and momentum. Moving to near Atlantic City, New Jersey, by eight p.m., the storm center was remaining just far enough offshore to prevent warm air from reaching the coast. As a result, it was drawing in copious amounts of moisture from the warm waters of the Gulf Stream and throwing a blanket of heavy snow that extended from Washington to New York.

Snow spread into New England late Saturday afternoon and advanced steadily north and east through the evening hours, reaching Boston shortly after seven-thirty, and Portsmouth, New Hampshire, before midnight. In Maine, Portland's first flakes fell around three o'clock Sunday morning, while at Bangor, daylight arrived shortly before the initial dusting commenced.

As the low continued to deepen Saturday night into Sunday, it set up an increasingly steep pressure gradient between itself and the retreating high to the northeast. A similar situation would likewise develop in the storm's wake, as the Arctic high spilling out of central Canada came roaring in to fill the void. The interaction created unusually heavy southeasterly to northeasterly gales across the entire North Atlantic coastal plain through much of Sunday, with central and southern New England bearing the brunt of the blow. Once the system passed, the winds swung into the northwest and reintensified, before slowly slackening from south to north on Monday.

Sunday morning, the monstrous ocean storm tracked across the elbow of Cape Cod. Continuing a northeasterly course, it reached Nova Scotia that night. As it pulled away from New England, a blast of the frigid Canadian air that had put the Midwestern states in the deep freeze surged in on blustery northwest gales, accompanied by occasional bursts of snow. Temperatures, which through Saturday had hovered in the upper twenties and low thirties across much of the six-state area, took a sharp nosedive. By Monday

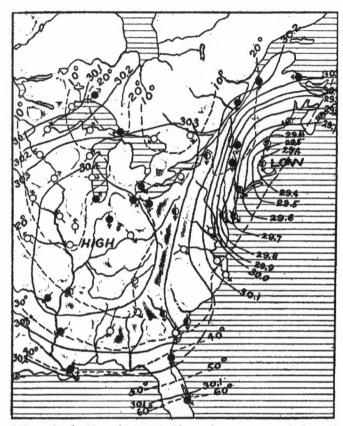

8:00 a.m., Sunday, November 27, 1898. The now huge ocean storm had moved to a position just south of Cape Cod. All but extreme southeastern New England was being buried beneath a blanket of ten to 40 inches of wind-whipped snows. At the coast, the morning high tide was accompanied by a powerful storm surge which rose over beaches and flooded extensive areas of the surrounding coastal plain.

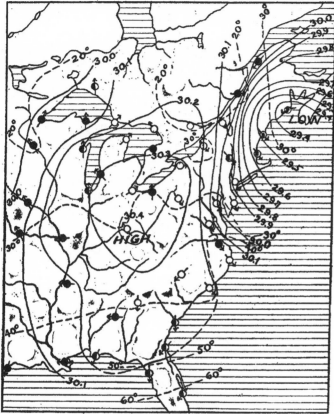

8:00 p.m., Sunday, November 27, 1898. As the great storm moved into the Canadian Maritimes, howling northwest winds in its wake ushered in a sharp blast of colder air which changed precipitation to snow in all areas and dropped temperatures an average of 25-30 degrees by Monday morning.

morning, most of the region was shivering from readings near or below zero.

In the days that lay ahead, residents shaking off the storm's effects would gradually come to learn what an extraordinary weather event they had endured and the extent of the disaster and devastation it had caused.

News traveled slowly at first and often came in bits and pieces. Across New England, the great winds had downed thousands of telephone and telegraph lines, effectively isolating many communities and preventing newspaper editors from picking up wire stories or gathering details from remote correspondents. Mail and passenger trains and coastal ferries, all of which resumed operations as quickly as conditions permitted, often carried the first, fragmentary intelligence from place to place.

In the absence of further word, storm coverage in the earliest papers was rudimentary, often little more than headlines. Succeeding editions added further particulars as quickly as additional reports were received. One of the stories slowest to unfold was also the deadliest and riveted the collective attention of New Englanders for days afterward. As evidence mounted that the steamer *Portland* and all aboard had been lost, each chilling revelation dominated all other storm-related features. Even after the likelihood of the vessel's sinking had become a certainty, controversy and speculation about major aspects of the tragedy continued well into December. And even then, many key questions remain unanswered.

THE PORTLAND SAGA
The Final, Fatal Voyage

On July 8, 1823, the 100-foot steamship *Patent* inaugurated marine passenger service between Boston and Portland. For nearly two decades afterward, a handful of small, ungainly vessels—among them: *Connecticut*, *Victory*, *Chancellor Livingston*, and *Portland*—linked Massachusetts waters with several Maine and New Brunswick communities, including Bath, Gardiner, Rockland, Bangor, and St. John.

While schedules were not always fixed, there was generally enough business to sustain more or less regular runs, even after competing companies came into being in the 1830s. The situation changed in November 1842, however, when the Boston and Maine railway system began offering rival service at lower fares and almost immediately lured countless travelers onto their trains. Rate wars ensued, although the steamship lines failed to entice enough patrons back to even pay the bills. It soon became evident they would have to work together to save themselves.

The owners consolidated their interests in 1844, forming the Portland Steam Packet Company, with working capital of $100,000. The firm built New England's first propeller-driven steamboats, *Commodore Preble* and *General Warren*, and used them to make three round trips a week between Portland and Boston. Touted as the "Propeller Line," the new firm charged riders only $1.00 each—a far

cry from the $5.00 fare commanded 15 years before. But even with the reduced rate, *Preble* and *Warren* survived only by hauling mostly freight. Through savvy management, strict attention to customer needs, continued modest rates, and much patience, the steamship firm gradually achieved a reputation for dependability, and passenger business ultimately returned.

With patrons again on the increase, PSP Co. added larger, more modern vessels to its fleet. First came the side-wheeler *John Marshall* in 1847, followed in the decade of the 1850s by several similar craft: *St. Lawrence*, *Atlantic*, *Forest City*, *Lewiston*, and *Montreal*. The latter ranged from 216 to 235 feet in length, although their modest beam engines—with 40- to 52-inch cylinders providing only 10- to 11-foot strokes—were generally considered underpowered for coastwise use.

Reviewing the first 20 years of operation, PSP Co's. annual report for 1863 proudly announced its boats had successfully completed 11,200 trips, safely delivering 1,400,000 passengers and 2,500,000 tons of freight in the process—a noteworthy record for the day.

Steam Packet officials subsequently placed even larger ships on the line. After dealing *Lewiston* to the Portland, Bar Harbor, and Machias Steamboat Company in 1867, and watching *Montreal* gutted by fire at its Portland wharf in August 1873, the firm commissioned a trio of side-wheelers: *Tremont*, in 1883; *Portland*, in 1890; and *Bay State*, in 1895. The latter, all-but-identical pair were the the firm's largest, most elegant creations to date—both constructed by the renowned New England Company of Bath.

CHAPTER TWO

Portland was designed by Bath architect William P. Pattee, and he and yard superintendent Amos B. Haggett took charge of the vessel's construction. Following the keel-laying in March 1889, New England Co. workers crafted a stout hull of white oak, yellow pine, and hackmatack, securely strapping the frame with iron belting. The vessel's convex sides, with long, sharp bow and tapering round stern, had been modeled in the yacht style.

Physically, *Portland* was an impressive ship, about 25 feet longer and more than 800 gross tons bulkier than *Tremont*. The sleek, white and gilt-trimmed hull measured 280.9 feet overall—nearly as long as a football field—and 42.1 feet across the beam. In fact, the maximum width was approximately 26 feet greater, because the ornate wooden guards shielding the paddle wheels protruded another 13 feet beyond either side of the hull. Within, a 225-foot-long main saloon and 400-ton freight capacity still left space for 168 staterooms and 234 berths. All told, *Portland* amply accommodated as many as 800 passengers.

Portland drew only 10 feet, eight inches of water, which suited it well for harbor travel and river passages, but was

One of the *Portland's* stateroom door number plaques.

less than ideal for oceangoing voyages. Nevertheless, contemporary mariners considered the vessel totally seaworthy. Powered by a walking beam engine with a 62-inch cylinder and 12-foot stroke capable of developing 1,500 horsepower at 50 pounds of pressure, the steamer would be able to attain a top speed of 13-14 knots.

Even as the steamship rose from the ways, the *Portland Evening Express* spoke glowingly about its construction and appearance and called attention to the many amenities designed expressly for the passengers' comfort, pleasure, and safety. Calling it "the finest vessel that will travel eastern waters," it lavished the following bits of praise in a September 1889 article:

> The bottom is solid timber as far as the turn of the bilge. She has two masts, schooner rig, and will carry sufficient sail to work her in case of accident to the machinery.
>
> The lower cabins, forward and aft of the engine, are separated by water-tight bulkheads. The forward cabin is used for a dining room. Both cabins are painted white with cherry trimmings. The main saloon is lighted with a dome sky-light. It is finished in the Corinthian style of architecture and furnished with richly carved mahogany furniture with wine colored plush upholstery. The floors are covered with velvet carpets.
>
> From the forward saloon by richly carved stairways, one ascends to the upper saloon, out of which are alcoves leading to 43 cool and airy rooms.

Portland on the ways at Bath, Maine.

Launching the steamer *Portland* on October 14, 1889.

Powerful steam pumps are provided in case of accident, either by fire or leakage, and the life saving service is perfect according to United States laws. There are 16 life boats and rafts, and 800 life preservers on board.

The bell, which is rung at the time of sailing, weighs 511 pounds...is hung on the frame of the walking beam.

The steamer *Portland* was launched October 14, 1889. After a noontime gathering of nearly 75 invited dignitaries at the neighboring Sagadahoc House, the select group rode in waiting carriages to the New England Company yard for a private tour of the new vessel. At 3:00 p.m., an assembled crowd of several hundred spectators watched in eager anticipation as workmen knocked away the stays holding the ship in place. As a tremor ran through the hull, Miss Emmie Coyle, daughter of PSP Co's. general manager James B. Coyle, christened *Portland* with a bottle of wine, and the handsome steamship slipped into the chilly waters of the Kennebec River. That fall and over the winter, the steamer's boilers, crafted at the Bath Iron Works, were installed; the machinery, from the Portland Company, set up; and the elaborate furnishings put in place.

Portland sailed on its maiden voyage Monday evening, June 14, 1890. The previous afternoon and evening, company officials proudly showed off the ship at a public open house. To the strains of music provided by Chandler's Band, an admiring crowd of several thousand—the local papers called it a "perfect crush"—swarmed over the vessel, delighting in the elegance that personified every inch of the ship.

A newspaper advertisement for the Portland Steamship Company service between Portland and Boston which featured *Bay State* and *Portland*.

The steamer *Portland* quickly gained a sterling reputation among those who traveled it—passengers and crew alike. In the spring of 1895, *Bay State* joined the line, and the kindred vessels ran opposite one another on the Portland-Boston route and developed a faithful clientele.

Until the time of its loss, *Portland* never suffered any serious mishaps. The closest call occurred September 8, 1895. That evening the ship collided with the Provincetown excursion steamer *Longfellow* off Rowe's Wharf, in Boston's inner harbor. *Portland* had just cleared India Wharf when it encountered the smaller, inbound ship. The 218-foot *Longfellow* sustained the brunt of the damage, although no one aboard either vessel was injured. *Portland* continued on to Maine as soon as the crew made ceratin there was no immediate danger to either craft.

Saturday morning, November 26, 1898, dawned sunny in Boston, with only a slight westerly breeze. As the morning wore on, however, the initial blue skies became veiled with high, thin cirrus clouds, causing the familiar "ring" around the sun, as its light was refracted by ice crystals in the overcast. It was Thanksgiving weekend, a time when families and friends traditionally congregate. That evening and the next would be unusually busy ones for the rail and steamship lines, as countless travelers bade farewell to loved ones before starting their return trips home.

At India Wharf, off the city's bustling Atlantic Avenue, the steamer *Portland* had been taking on a cargo consisting of 100 tons of general freight, mostly destined for Maine merchants and businesses anticipating the upcoming Christmas season. The steamship had arrived the previous afternoon from Portland, where first mate Edward B. Deering supervised the fueling for the upcoming round

A metal tag from a passenger's baggage.

trip. Workers at Randall & McAllister Coal Co. had topped off the vessel's bunkers with 81 tons of coal, besides filling each of two, one-ton compartments and placing another seven tons on deck. Deering wanted to make certain the big ship was fully coaled, because he would not be making the return trip. He and two of his colleagues, first pilot Louis F. Strout and purser's mate J.F. Hunt, had gotten Captain Blanchard's permission to remain in Boston and attend the funeral of Captain Charles Deering. The former skipper of *Bay State* had died Thanksgiving night, and the funeral would be held Sunday, the 27th.

Captain Deering's death was the second, related blow to the steamship line that month. On November 7, John B. Coyle, Jr., the company's general manager, had also passed away, prompting the firm to promote Boston agent John F. Liscomb to the post. With Captain Deering now gone, PSC had just named Alexander Dennison, *Bay State's* first pilot, as that ship's next master. It meant *Bay State* would be operating with a newly appointed captain and novice first pilot, as well.

During Saturday afternoon, the high clouds over Boston thickened and lowered, although the weather remained placid and serene. As was his habit, *Portland's* skipper, Captain Hollis H. Blanchard, went to the Weather Bureau office downtown to check the latest weather maps and forecasts and chat with John W. Smith, the meteorologist-in-charge. During the visit, Blanchard learned that the previous day's area of storminess over the Great Lakes was apparently transferring its energy to a deepening secondary storm off the mid-Atlantic coast. This development had caused the Bureau's headquarters in Washington to rush out a special advisory for heavy snow over New England, beginning Saturday night and lasting into Sunday.

As daytime faded into evening darkness, Blanchard must have thought long and hard about whether he should make the overnight trip to Portland. In his mid-fifties, he had worked for the line—the company had recently changed its name from Portland Steam Packet Company to Portland Steamship Company—for more than eight years, including a stint as pilot aboard *Bay State*. A family man, he lived in Deering, a Portland suburb, with a wife, son, and 19-year old daughter; a second son was then residing in Boston. Blanchard would want to spend time with them when he could, yet he fully realized his responsibility as master of his own vessel, a position he had worked diligently to earn. He must put the interests and safety of his passengers, crew, and vessel ahead of his own.

Promptly at 7:00 p.m., *Portland* cast off its lines and slipped from India Wharf, to begin the overnight, 100-mile passage to Portland—a destination the steamship would never reach.

✳

According to numerous eyewitnesses, the early portion of Portland's final trip was routine and uneventful. Those aboard several passing vessels—and at least one onshore

Captain Hollis H. Blanchard

The keeper of Deer Island Light observed the *Portland's* passage out of Boston Harbor.

observer—reported seeing the ship as it sailed down Boston Harbor. One was Kennebec, another Bath-built steamship, which had earlier cast off for Gardiner, Maine. After putting to sea, Captain Jason Collins decided not to make the trip and brought the vessel back to Boston harbor. Kennebec lay anchored in President Roads, between Long and Deer Islands, when the larger Portland glided past—shortly before seven-thirty. Captain Collins supposedly whistled at the outbound vessel, in what some have claimed was a gesture of warning, but received no response.

About the same time, Deer Island Light keeper Wesley Pingree watched *Portland* as it slipped past his station. Those aboard the Boston pilot boat *Sylph*, headed in from the vicinity of the Boston lightship, likewise saw the steamer as it exited the harbor. Also prior to eight o'clock, the Boston-bound *Mt. Desert*, yet another Maine-based passenger steamer, encountered *Portland* when the latter was about a mile west of Graves Light.

Moments later, Captain Charles T. Martell of the tug *Channing* met the steamship at close range. Martell later commented:

> "I was steering…in a southeasterly direction… We were off Nahant. The weather was not bad at the time, but I knew a serious storm was coming. There were 10 or 12 young men gathered on the topside of the *Portland*, just forward and aft of the paddle-wheel box. When one of the young bloods on the *Portland* shouted across to me to get my old scow out of the way, I shouted back

to him, 'You'd better stop that hollering, because I don't think you'll be this smart tomorrow morning. By this time I was less than 20 feet from the *Portland* and could easily make out the features of the young men sailing to their death. I gave three blasts of the *Channing's* whistle, and Captain Blanchard, whom I could easily recognize in the wheel house, answered back."

Between nine and ten p.m., other south-bound vessels scurrying for port reported meeting the big steamship on its way north. Captain William Thomas, of the fishing schooner *Maude S.*, spotted *Portland's* lights when he was off Bass Rocks, southwest of Thacher's Island. Thomas had more than a casual interest in the steamer that evening; he believed his wife was aboard. As it turned out, she had changed her mind and did not sail.

The crew of the two-masted schooner *Windward*, making for Boston, likewise related seeing *Portland* in the same general area. Its captain, William D. Scott, later recalled, "We were so close to the vessel that the passengers called to us from the deck...and we could hear them plainly. The sea was very calm, but we knew we had a bad night ahead of us..." *Windward* reached Boston safely, but only after a frightful trip. Captain Scott's son Charles was aboard that night and remembered that the storm engulfed them soon after they met *Portland*. He recounted how he and his father lashed themselves to the schooner's helm to avoid

being washed overboard.

Portland reached Thacher's Island, off the eastern tip of the Cape Ann peninsula, prior to ten p.m. Keeper Addison Franklin Tarr of the twin-towered Thacher's Island lighthouses later testified that weather conditions were so good at the time the steamship would normally have passed the station—between nine-thirty and ten o'clock—he made no attempt to note the occasion and never did see the ship go by. However, Albert L. Whitten, one of Tarr's assistants, did witness the steamer from the lens room of the north light tower.

Captain Lynes B. Hathaway, master workman for the U.S. Lighthouse Service and staying at the Thacher's Island station that night, told Boston newspapers that he, too, watched *Portland's* lights as the ship steamed past, coming within 500 feet of Thacher's eastern shore sometime after nine-thirty. He said the vessel sailed between it and the Londoner, a dangerous, partially submerged reef about a half mile southeast of the island, and he witnessed nothing unusual. Hathaway's associate, William Harrington, was with him at the time and corroborated the story.

Before midnight, snow overspread Boston's north shore communities and the coastal waters from Salem to Gloucester, quickly reducing visibility and making further sightings of *Portland* less likely and more difficult to pinpoint. Nonetheless, three more were reported in Boston

WILLIAM SCOTT

A detail of a painting by noted marine artist Raymond Prosser, showing the meeting of the steamer *Portland* and the schooner *Grayling* off Cape Ann on the evening of November 26, 1898.

newspapers. Unfortunately, they create more confusion than they explain. At best, they raise reasonable doubt that *Portland* ever got much further north than Thacher's Island.

The *Boston Herald* recounted that around eleven p.m. Captain Reuben Cameron, aboard the schooner *Grayling*, spotted a steamship 12 miles south by east of Thacher's Island. Cameron said the vessel, which he felt certain was *Portland*, was bearing down on his own craft and came so close that he burned a flare to warn it away. Cameron claimed he could see nothing physically wrong with the larger ship, although it was rolling and pitching considerably.

According to the *Boston Daily Advertiser*, the Gloucester-bound schooner *Florence E. Stream* encountered a paddle-wheel steamer on a westerly heading, within minutes of Captain Cameron's sighting. The vessel's skipper, Captain Frank Stream, could not absolutely identify the ship, but assumed it was *Portland*, because he figured it was the only vessel of that type likely to be anywhere in the vicinity at the time.

No more than a half hour later, Captain D.J. Pellier, aboard the fishing schooner *Edgar Randall*, claimed he saw a large vessel running without lights, bearing down on him at a point roughly 14 miles east-southeast of Eastern Point, Gloucester. Pellier said he swung the little schooner away, to avoid being run into. As he did, he could make out a paddle-wheel steamer with a badly damaged superstructure and he presumed it was *Portland*. In the *Boston Globe's* account of the incident, Pellier is cited as saying the vessel was laboring heavily and making relatively little headway, although it showed no rockets or other signals of distress. He is also quoted as adding he believed that *Portland* broke down off Thacher's.

In Thomas Harrison Eames' popular 1940 chronicle of the *Portland* sinking, he hypothesizes that the steamship:

> ...may have had a mechanical breakdown and attempted to run into Gloucester, as suggested by her apparently westerly course when she passed the Stream; or her engines may have been disabled temporarily and allowed the northeasterly seas to swing her around into the trough so that she headed in a more or less northwesterly direction.

There is no apparent evidence that *Portland* was sighted again that night. Those who have studied the storm and its aftermath over the years generally agree that the powerful winds and mountainous seas during the early hours of Sunday morning eventually overpowered the vessel and forced it gradually southward across Massachusetts Bay.

Snow flurries reached Maine after midnight Saturday and began falling steadily in Portland shortly after three a.m. Sunday, less than two hours before *Portland* was due. At the Steamship Company office on Franklin Wharf, little concern was shown when the vessel failed to arrive on schedule. Contrary winds and inclement weather might have caused the ship to slow, and in such cases the trip could take as much as an extra hour or two—sometimes more. Besides, there was no certainty the ship had ever left Boston.

By six a.m., it was snowing heavily across the city. At the

Weather Bureau office on Exchange Street, just up the rise from the waterfront, observers measured the northeast wind at 42 miles an hour. Considering the reading was taken at a relatively sheltered spot, Bureau chief E.P. Jones claimed it might have then been blowing as much as 20 miles an hour harder outside the harbor.

While southern Maine was only then realizing the storm's first effects, it was nearing its maximum intensity over Cape Cod. During the night, sustained winds near Highland Light had been clocked at near hurricane force, with gusts approaching 90 miles an hour. At 5:45 a.m., Keeper Samuel O. Fisher of the Race Point Life-Saving Station, four miles north of Provincetown, heard four short blasts from a steamer's whistle[1]. Alerting the station crew, he phoned the Peaked Hill Bars station, some four miles to the east, then sent one of his men onto the beach to look for a vessel in distress. Fisher's handwritten notation of the incident appears in the station's daily journal:

> At 5:45 a.m. I heard Stmr. blow four whistles distress signal. Called my crew. Sent No. 1 (surfman John Johnson) out. Expected to find Stmr. close to station. Got horse harnessed and beach apparatus ready for a jump. Telephoned to Keeper of PH (Peaked Hill) Bar (Life-Saving Station) to have his crew ready for a jump and we all looked for the Stmr. but could find no trace of her, no drift (wreckage) or anything.

By mid-morning, a surprising lull in the storm occurred

Searching for possible shipwrecks and shipwreck survivors, a Cape Cod surfman patrols the shoreline.

[1] The news of Fisher's observation traveled fast. Lloyd's of London in a special report on the *Portland* sinking, related Fisher had heard four short blasts.

The former gunboat *Pentagoet* might have been one of the two steamships seen off Cape Cod by Captain Michael Francis Hogan of the fishing boat *Ruth M. Martin* during a break in the gale Sunday morning. Hogan reported seeing both a paddle-wheel steamer, which he believed to be *Portland*, and a propeller-driven vessel. The steam screw *Pentagoet* was lost in the storm, and several pieces of wreckage having a distinctive, red color, which was peculiar to this Civil War-era ship, were subsequently found amidst *Portland* wreckage on the beaches of the Outer Cape.

over Cape Cod Bay and portions of the outer Cape. The visibility improved, the howling winds moderated, and the sun actually broke through the clouds for a short time. Some writers have suggested the "eye" of the storm—such is found in a well-developed hurricane—was passing overhead. Today's meteorologists explain how tightly wound ocean storms typically draw a "dry slot" into the inner circulation. Within this sector, precipitation stops, the wind may slacken appreciably, and breaks in the clouds sometimes occur. It is this weather phenomenon that created the unexpected weather change.

Second District (Cape Cod) Life-Saving Service Superintendent Benjamin C. Sparrow wrote a January 25, 1899, letter to William A. Swan of the Associated Press in Boston, in which he described the suddenly improving weather picture on the Outer Cape:

> ...a partial breaking up of the gale the wind became moderate, the sun shone for a short time and the atmosphere cleared to an extent which disclosed two coastwise steamers passing southward, also a fishing schooner lying to under short sail, all of which was reported by telephone to this office... about 11 o'clock the gale again increased and vision was obscure from the offing until after daylight on Monday morning...

The fishing schooner that Superintendent Sparrow mentioned was *Ruth M. Martin*, then in distress four miles off Highland Light. The 89-foot vessel had spent a fearful night working northward from a point off Chatham Light late Saturday. The furious winds had tattered the vessel's sails,

and monstrous seas carried away the boats and anchors. The schooner's captain, Michael Francis Hogan, had been trying to reach the comparative safety of Provincetown harbor, but was becoming increasingly concerned the little schooner would not hold together until he did.

Between eight and nine a.m., Captain Hogan and the crew spotted a "large side-wheel steamer" about a mile to the southeast, which they were sure was *Portland*. Hogan said it appeared to be drifting with the wind, but was keeping its head to the storm, indicating it was under power. He claimed that he and the men kept the ship in view for about two hours, until they drifted so far apart the returning stormy weather and reduced visibility caused it to fade from view.

About the same time, *Martin's* crew also made out a screw steamship to leeward. Ordering his mate, Patrick Droohan, to place a distress flag in the schooner's rigging, Captain Hogan hoped to attract the unknown vessel's attention. But the signal went unheeded, and Hogan ultimately was able to weather the Cape on his own and beach the hapless schooner in Provincetown's inner harbor, just as it began breaking up.

Ruth M. Martin was later hauled free and patched up, and Captain Hogan jury-rigged and sailed it to Boston for repairs. Quizzed there about whether it was actually *Portland* he had sighted off the Cape, Hogan told *Boston Herald* reporters he "was well acquainted" with the steamship and felt certain it was the vessel they had seen.

Hogan also suggested the propeller-driven steamer he had witnessed might have been *Pentagoet*, a Civil War-era,

Captain Hogan could also have possibly seen the propeller-driven *Horatio Hall* off Cape Cod. Feared lost in the storm, the *Horatio Hall* survived the storm by heaving to and turning its bow to the wind 40 miles east of Thacher's Island. Even so, the passenger steamer could have been beaten far to the south during the night and been off the northern tip of Cape Cod the next morning.

converted gunboat hauling passengers and freight for the Manhattan Steamship Company. The 128-foot vessel had left New York Saturday morning, bound for Rockland and Bangor. Observers on shore near Highland Light sighted *Pentagoet* Saturday afternoon on the vessel's northward trek, and Captain Pye of the steamer *Halifax* reported passing it about six p.m., north of Boston. Newspaper accounts in the days following the storm speculated the 34-year-old ship may have gotten as far north as the Maine coast Saturday night before being forced back, as *Portland* apparently was. Scattered bits of wreckage presumed to be from *Pentagoet* because of their unusual red coloring were ultimately discovered on the beaches from North Truro to Nauset.

The Maine Steamship Company's new passenger steamer *Horatio Hall* is another, though less likely candidate to be the mysterious steamship seen from *Ruth M. Martin.* Under the command of Captain Albert Bragg, the 297-foot liner had sailed from Portland at 8:00 p.m., Saturday, bound for New York. According to his statement, given at the *Portland* examination the following spring, Captain Bragg encountered the storm later that night, when *Horatio Hall* was some 40 miles east of Thacher's Island. Conditions soon became so violent, Bragg hove the ship to after midnight, holding the bow into the wind until nearly eight o'clock Sunday morning. Even so, *Horatio Hall* could have been beaten that far south during the night and been off the northern tip of Cape Cod when the visibility improved.

The savage storm pulled away from Cape Cod ever so slowly Sunday afternoon and evening. Rain and snow, driven on by near hurricane force winds, continued to sweep across the sandy peninsula the rest of the day, before abating overnight.

That evening, surfman John J. Johnson of the Peaked Hill Bars Life-Saving Station was walking the shore west of the station. Johnson had just met fellow watchman George Henry Bickers of the Race Point station at the halfway house between the two outposts and was on his way east, back to his own place. Shortly before seven-thirty, he spied a small object in the wash, tossed up by the heavy surf. It was a life belt emblazoned with the words "Str. *Portland.*" While it was no proof the big steamship was close by or necessarily in trouble, the unusual find prompted Johnson to scan the shoreline and incoming breakers with even greater regard as he made his way along the beach.

Moments later, almost in front of his own station, Johnson spotted a large Turner Center (Maine) Creamery milk can bobbing and tossing in the surf—and in the next few moments, nearly a dozen others like it. In his own words:

Formerly used as a warning sign on *Portland*, this sign washed ashore on Cape Cod.

Surfman Gideon Bowley, patroling the beach near the High Head Life-Saving Station, discovers the body of a black man wearing a life preserver labeled "*Str. Portland.*"

FOUR SHORT BLASTS

I was bound west toward the station, when I found the first thing that landed from the steamer. It was a life belt and it was one-half mile east of the station. At 7:45 o'clock that evening I found the next seen wreckage, a creamery can, forty quart, I guess. It was right below our station, and nine or ten more of them, all empty and stoppered tightly came on there closely together. Jim Kelley succeeded me on the eastern beat, leaving the station at 8:20 p.m., and at 9:30, he found doors and other light woodwork from the Portland on the shore,. When I found the life belt, the wind was northeast.

Around eleven p.m., near the time of high tide, wreckage clearly identifiable as belonging to *Portland* began coming ashore in large quantities. Most was clustered in a half-mile stretch between the Race Point and Peaked Hill Bars stations. Edwin B. Tyler, of the Race Point crew, found doors, electric light bulbs, washstand tops, and other items. Within an hour, the beach was littered with *Portland* debris. The midnight watch from Race Point likewise discovered tangled masses of rubble—mattresses, chairs, upholstery, windows, and paneling—tumbling ashore. By now, it seemed painfully evident that *Portland* had foundered somewhere off the stormy cape, and as the night wore on more and more evidence of Steamer *Portland's* demise piled up along the Outer Cape.

The fragmentary remains the life-savers had found were sobering, but not as much so as the ones in the wee hours of Monday morning. At 2:20 a.m., Gideon Bowley, No. 1 surfman at High Head, was about a half mile west of the station when he came upon the body of a black man wearing a life belt belonging to the steamer *Portland*. Summoning his mates, Bowley and members of the Highland station moved the corpse above the reach of the tides before beginning a search for other victims.

Keeper Edwin P. Worthen of the Highland station noted the incident in his log for Monday, November 28:

> At 4 a.m., surfman No. 3 (J. Marshall) called the keeper (Worthen) and said there was wreckage coming ashore. All hands were called, half going each way along the beach. Keeper with surfman Nos. 1, 4, and 5 went towards the (Highland) light; when abreast of it found some wreckage, and on looking around saw something up close to the bank. On going to it, found it to be a man with a life belt on, plainly marked 'Steamer Portland.' We carried the man along shore until we came to a place where we could leave him with safety, then went for an undertaker, there being no coroner within a reasonable distance.

After daylight, other crews located more bodies, including one of a woman near the Highland station and a man near the Pamet River. By nightfall, more than a dozen *Portland* victims had washed ashore—from Race Point to Nauset. During the next three days, the total climbed to 21, as additional finds were made at Wellfleet and Nauset.

On December 3, a flask containing a message supposedly from Captain Blanchard was picked up on the beach nearly opposite White Head, Nantasket Beach. It read:

> Help! On board the *Portland*. We are sinking. Upper works gone, two miles off Highland Light. Time, 7:30 Sunday. Blanchard

A surfman drags a body from the the rolling waves.

The report received little attention and no credence.

Then in early May 1899, George B. Leonard picked up an empty quart bottle floating in the water off Cliff Island, Maine. Inside was a scrap of paper which began: 'November 27, on board the steamer *Portland*.' It briefly mentioned that the vessel's superstructure was gone and the crew expected the ship to go down in a short time. The vessel's location was simply given as southeast of Thacher's Island. The note was unsigned.

Some Cliff Island residents actually believed the message was legitimate. Others felt a more likely explanation was that somebody, after consuming the contents of the bottle, decided it would be a good joke to write the note, place it inside, and throw it into the ocean.

On December 4, another powerful northeast storm raked the New England coast. Angry seas tossed up more *Portland* victims and uncovered several others previously on shore, but already buried in the ever-shifting sands. Three days later, the *Boston Globe* reported the body count had reached 35. With one exception, all the corpses uncovered by the December storm were located between Orleans and Monomoy—30 to 60 miles south of where Gideon Bowley had encountered the initial one.

The grim finds continued every so often for weeks afterward. Just before Christmas, Keeper Lewis of the Nauset Beach lighthouses at Eastham came upon a badly decomposed body near the station, exposed by a storm two days before. On January 8, 1899, a surfman from the Old Harbor crew in Chatham pulled the battered remains of a man

Working to identify a body at Orleans.

from the surf, just north of the station.

As corpses were recovered, they were taken to nearby funeral homes or placed in makeshift morgues—including Mayo's blacksmith shop and the railroad station in Orleans. Undertakers in Provincetown, Wellfleet, Orleans, and Chatham were temporarily overwhelmed by the sudden deluge of bodies, to say nothing of the widespread attention from newspaper reporters, the constant comings and goings of bereaved individuals searching for lost family members—and the just plain curious.

Nearly all the victims that came ashore were eventually identified, although a few were too badly maimed or mutilated to be recognizable. Medical examiner Dr. Samuel T. Davis of Orleans supervised the identification of corpses, aided by photographs which steamship company agent Charles F. Williams requested and received from friends and relatives of the dead. To aid the recognition process, the victims were each described in detail, according to their physical features, clothing, personal possessions, etc. One profile read:

> Body A 5: ...5 feet, 11 inches, about 45 years of age, blue cheviot suit, striped trousers, four-in-hand necktie with small Masonic pin, small plain gold band ring in pocket, slate colored underclothing, leather pocket book with three $1 bills and a silver dollar, two tortoise shell pocket knives, celluloid collars and cuffs, sleeve buttons with mosaic stones, ring on little finger of right hand with onyx stone, heavy reddish mustache running to the ears, that is, mustache and side whiskers meet in an odd way, bald nearly to the crown of the head, hair black and cut short, russet shoes, black stockings, remains of a watch found in side coat pocket, works gone, one door key, one small key.

HER DEATH ROLL FOREVER A SECRET.

Portland's Victims Being Carried Away by Ocean Currents.

A shocking *Boston Herald* headline warns relatives that their loved-ones bodies are being swept into eternity.

On December 3, the Commonwealth of Massachusetts took formal charge of the post-mortem process. All bodies not already en route to next-of-kin were shipped to the North Grove Street Mortuary or City Hospital in Boston, where they were photographed and embalmed, while arrangements were made to have them sent on to relatives, for services and burial.

As more and more victims were identified, a revealing cross-section of passengers and crew began to emerge. The large majority of passengers were Maine people, most from greater Portland. Many were returning from Thanksgiving celebrations with families and friends in the Boston area.

Several were young professional women—among them, at least three teachers. Susan A. Kelley, 21, had recently completed studies in Europe and accepted a position in

Charles H. Thompson, his wife Susie, and their daughter Gladys, residents of Portland's Woodfords section, were lost when *Portland* foundered off Cape Cod.

the language department at Portland High School. Sophie B. Holmes, 33, had started her fifth year at the North School in Portland. Helen M. Langthorne, after several years at the Brackett Street School, had decided to teach music in the Deering public schools.

Two others had worked as clerks at the Owen, Moore & Co. department store on Congress Street. Maude Sykes was returning to resume her duties, while Emily L. Cobb had recently resigned to pursue her musical ambitions as a soprano. In fact, Emily was hurrying back to sing in Portland's First Parish Church choir on Sunday morning. Maude had recently endured a personal tragedy; her fiance, Portland

soldier Charles Lovell, had been killed the previous summer during the Spanish-American War.

Others had quite different reasons for making the weekend voyage. Aspiring artist Henry de Merritt Young was en route to Portland for the first public exhibit of his paintings—watercolors which depicted the Massachusetts north shore and the Maine coast. Mrs. Cornelia Mitchell had less cheerful business; she had just received a telegram that a relative had passed away and was planning to attend the funeral.

Mrs. Miranda Safford of Portland was headed home after visiting her ailing brother, C.F. Elswell, of Beachmont. Before boarding the boat at Portland, she had a premonition she would never return and almost decided not to leave. Her friends laughed at her fears and prevailed on her to go. Eva Totten of Cambridge had originally planned to leave the following Monday, but her desire to be with her ill mother in Portland prompted her to start sooner.

Not all the victims were traveling alone. A few youthful fathers had sons or daughters in tow; others,

The bodies of the Thompson family never came ashore; however, their deaths have been memorialized on the Day family stone in a New Gloucester, Maine, cemetery.

entire families. Oren Hooper was accompanied by his 13-year old son Carl; William L. Chase, by 12-year old Philip; Louis Silverstaine, by 6-year old Harry. Charles H. Thompson, manager of the C.H. Thompson grocery store in the Woodfords section of Portland, had his wife Susan and three-year old daughter Gladys with him. Jes Jessen Schmidt and his wife Jessine were returning to Portland with their two children, Jorgen Jessen, 5, and Anton, 4, following an extended trip to the parents' native Denmark.

While most were ordinary citizens, a few had fashioned distinguished careers. The Honorable E. Dudley Freeman, a prominent Yarmouth attorney and state senator, had served as chairman of the governor's council in Augusta. James Flower was a graduate of Harvard College and Boston University School of Law. Just

Second Steward
Francis Eben Heuston
of Portland.

two weeks before the ill-fated trip, he had moved from St. John, New Brunswick, to accept the president's post at Bliss Business College in Lewiston.

Many of *Portland's* officers and crew had spent their professional lives at sea, and several were popular, well-respected, veteran employees. Stewardess Mrs. Carrie E. Harris, second pilot Lewis Nelson, purser Frederick A. Ingraham, waiter W.H. Cash, and fireman Hugh Merriman were among the senior employees—Harris, Ingra-ham, and Merriman each having served the line some 20 years.

While the several life-saving crews were the first to know the sad news of *Portland's* fate, it would be almost two days before the outside world learned of the tragedy. All lines of communication to and from Cape Cod had effectively been cut off, so those who knew the story had no way to tell anyone else. The high winds had downed countless telephone and telegraph lines. Flooding rains had undermined the

Jennie G. Edmonds
of East Boston.

railroad tracks leaving Provincetown and washed away three or four miles of roadbed between West Barnstable and Sagamore. Through the day Monday, the still-tumultuous seas prevented boats from venturing out of harbors.

At Portland, steamship officials comforted themselves Sunday morning with the assumption that *Portland* had stayed in port. Later in the day they exchanged news with general manager Liscomb in Boston, so both knew the ship had sailed as scheduled, but hadn't arrived in Maine. The company's best remaining hope was that it had found a temporary safe haven or ridden out the blow at sea.

Hampered by phone outages, Liscomb tried repeatedly to contact ports where *Portland* might have sought refuge. Around four p.m., he was able to get through to Gloucester, only to learn the big ship had not put in there. Still hopeful the vessel would eventually show up safe and sound, he

Throngs of anxious relatives and co-workers crowded the offices of the Portland Steamship Company in Boston and Portland seeking word of the fate of *Portland*'s passengers and crew.

issued a statement that appeared in the Monday morning edition of the *Boston Journal*:

> Note: People having friends on board the steamer Portland...should not become alarmed for the safety of the vessel as yet. Telephone and telegraphic communications with ports along the north shore .is entirely cut off, and for that reason no word can be obtained as to the Portland's whereabouts.
>
> It is not unlikely that the big steamer headed back for Boston when she ran into the storm Saturday night and is now anchored in a sheltered spot down the harbor, for no tugs dared ventured very far down on Sunday, and, owning to falling snow, a good view of what was down below could not be obtained.

Around ten o'clock that night, Liscomb gave up trying to find the missing steamship on his own and made arrangements to have the revenue cutters *Woodbury*, out of Portland, and *Dallas*, from Boston, conduct a search at sea.

Meanwhile, others were growing increasingly concened about *Portland's* whereabouts. Sunday into Monday, friends and relatives of ones thought to have sailed, showed up at the steamship company offices in both Portland and Boston, nervously awaiting any news. Sympathetic employees could offer no information, even about who was aboard; the only passenger list was on the ship. In light of the throngs congregating on its doorsteps in both cities, the company soon realized that its assumption of only 25 to 35 was far too conservative. It revised the figure upward several times, eventually deciding it was in excess of

Seeking a missing relative, a black woman told shipping company officials, "He was a cook, Sir."

100 hundred passengers.

Around two p.m. Monday, the steamer *Bay State* arrived at India Wharf, following a rough, but uneventful passage from Maine. Although passengers and crew had watched the seas intently as the vessel came along, no one saw any sign of the still-missing *Portland*. After *Bay State* docked and unloaded, PSC management opened the ship's saloon to the waiting crowds, many of whom had been shivering in the cold for hours. The firm also kept its offices open through the night, so employees could immediately pass on any late word of the steamer's fate.

Monday afternoon, the *Boston Herald's* Chatham correspondent Charles F. Ward was at Hyannis, when he received part of a telegraph message from an assistant in Truro. The wire went dead in the middle of the transmission, but not until Ward learned that wreckage and bodies from *Portland* had come ashore the previous night between Provincetown and Truro.

Unable to get the startling revelation through to the *Herald's* Boston offices, Ward got aboard a work train leaving Hyannis at 6:30 that evening and rode as far as East Sandwich, where the tracks had washed out. Determined he would get the mo-

The steamer *Bay State* tied up at Boston's India Wharf and reported it had seen no sign of the missing *Portland* on its run down the coast.

ALL PERISHED !

The Steamer Portland Carried 140 Souls to Death on Cape Cod.

Wrecked at 10 A. M. Sunday—Names of the Lost—Herald First with the News.

The *Boston Herald's* bold headline tells it all.

Hoping for the best and fearing the worst, bereaved friends and relatives arrive in Orleans,.

to steamship company agent Williams. By evening, newspaper headlines across the city screamed the worst—the steamer *Portland* had foundered and all on board were feared lost!

Over the years, assertions have been made that word of the Portland disaster was first flashed to Boston via transatlantic cable—from Orleans, Massachusetts, to Paris, France, then on to Newfoundland, Canada, and finally to Boston. According to the *Boston Globe*, however, the storm knocked the cable out of service from November 27 until December 3, and thus the *Herald's* Charles F. Ward rightly deserves the distinction of being the initial bearer of the sad tidings.

mentous story to the newspaper at the earliest possible moment, Ward started walking through the slush and snow toward Sandwich. Arriving around eleven p.m., he hired a horse and rode another nine miles to Buzzards Bay, where the tracks were open to Boston. He then boarded the next available train, arriving in the city around mid-morning with the first shocking news of the disaster.

Tuesday forenoon, a *Herald* official relayed the grim news

Disaster and Devastation At Sea

For all the destruction and suffering it caused across the northeastern United States, the great *Portland* Gale was most deadly at sea. It developed rapidly and overspread the New England coastal plain during the nighttime hours, when darkness made its arrival and intensity less discernible and all the more difficult to escape. Spawning winds of greater than hurricane force which ripped across Massachusetts Bay and the vast shoal waters south and east of Cape Cod, it churned up 30- and 40-foot seas, and literally overwhelmed shipping with little or no warning.

As it became evident this was no ordinary weather event, scores of smaller vessels went scrambling for the nearest safe haven, while larger ships and those farther offshore did their best to weather the blow at sea. Some escaped the fury; many more did not. In its wake, the savage storm left hundreds of miles of shore strewn with dozens of wrecked or disabled craft. A smaller, though considerable number foundered at sea.

Even before the howling northeast winds slackened and the monstrous seas subsided, the coastline from Long Island to Penobscot Bay revealed graphic evidence of the storm's fury. Splintered and shattered hulks sprawled uncharacteristically against ledges, canted against or atop wharves, or perched high on beaches, far above the ocean's normal reach. The broken masts and tattered sails of others protruded from partially sunken hulls, or unceremoniously cluttered harbor bottoms. Few escaped unharmed.

Along the Connecticut and Rhode Island coasts, whose indented river and seaports show a southerly exposure, losses were significant, although less catastrophic than in other areas. Along the Thames River at New London, several small boats were upset and larger ones driven against piers. Others were damaged after dragging their anchors into shoal waters. South of Providence, 51 vessels were reported ashore along the western shores of Narragansett Bay, although many suffered only minor damage.

Offshore, it was a different story. At Block Island, the storm was the worst in the memory of the oldest fisherman. The wind speed officially reached 90 miles per hour Sunday morning, before the anemometer measuring it was torn from the top of the U.S. Weather Bureau office and blown into the sea. Observers at the station estimated the force later reached 110 m.p.h. Crews from the New Shoreham Life-Saving Station, near the landing on the east side of the island, rescued or cared for about 40 shipwrecked mariners. The island's entire fishing fleet of 24 vessels was considered a total loss—the majority tossed on shore and battered to pieces. Some simply sank at their moorings when the extreme tides pulled them beneath the surface. Vessels in the old harbor fared a bit better, though most were badly damaged after colliding with one another.

The storm track followed a course over southeastern Massachusetts, where marine commerce suffered untold damage. Of the 50 vessels which sought refuge at Vine-

Chapter Three

yard Haven, on the north shore of Martha's Vineyard, only five escaped unharmed. By midnight Saturday, sustained winds had reached 60 miles per hour; for several hours Sunday early morning, they were well above hurricane force. The two-masted schooner *Island City* drove ashore at two a.m. Sunday, between the wharves at Cottage City. Before help could reach the stricken sailors, all five perished. One man froze to death and was found hanging from the rigging by his heels. At Gay Head, on the western side of the island, life-saving crews and local fishermen battled the elements for 29 hours before rescuing six of the seven mariners trapped aboard a three-masted schooner which had anchored in Menemsha Bight. As the gale strengthened Saturday night, the helpless vessel was pushed into perilous shallows some 600 yards from the beach. A second, larger schooner suffered the same plight and was dashed to pieces, killing six of the crew before anyone else knew what had happened.

The majority of the seven hardy lightships standing on the shoal waters in and around Nantucket Sound also suffered the effects of the monster storm. The Hen and Chickens lightship, *No. 2*, normally moored at the entrance to Buzzard's Bay, went adrift and couldn't be located for nearly a week. It was eventually spotted, nearly 25 miles southeast of Nantucket. The Handkerchief lightship, *No. 4*, drifted more than four miles from its customary spot, southwest of Monomoy Point. The ship's massive iron anchor broke free and only the long length of heavy, connecting chain—acting as a sea anchor—kept the vessel from straying further. The lighthouse tender *Azalea* towed

The schooner *King Philip* was lost with all hands during the great November gale of 1898.

the ship to Hyannis harbor for a replacement fluke, before heading to sea again to retrieve the Pollock Rip light-vessel. *No. 47* broke free from its normal post, southeast of Monomoy, and drifted to the Delaware breakwater.

Nearly 50 vessels were ultimately reported lost off the great beaches and harbors of Cape Cod. For days afterward, tangled masses of wreckage washed ashore from Provincetown to Chatham, giving occasional clues to the fate of ships which had met their untimely end at sea. Scattered bits and pieces of the four-masted schooner *King Philip* and the coastwise steamship *Pentagoet* added to the mysteries of how and where these craft had been lost. Among the rubble were portions of superstructure and cargo from the fashionable Boston-Portland steamer *Port-*

The schooner *Canaria* and other damaged vessels in Vineyard Haven.

land. As nothing else could, the shocking discoveries of three dozen bodies identified as among *Portland's* 190-plus victims, underscored the magnitude of devastation wrought by the blow.

No fewer than 27 schooners attempted to ride out the storm at Provincetown, which forms the northernmost curl of the outer Cape. The bustling fishing community encompasses a spacious harbor that is considered one of the safest on the Atlantic coast during northerly and easterly storms. But even here, the great gale had far-reaching effects. Before wind and wave subsided Sunday night, ten large vessels and several smaller craft had come ashore. Several foundered at their anchors or drifted into shallow water, where their keels pounded on the bottom until the seams opened and waterlogged them. Others were lifted high and dry by the tides. One fishing boat was found on its side, more than 100 feet above the everyday high-water mark.

A vessel ashore at Plymouth

Early Sunday, the schooners *Jordan L. Mott* and *Lester L. Lewis* went ashore between Long Point lighthouse and the Wood End Life-Saving Station. The two-masted *Mott* sank just off the bar, with the boiling surf covering all but the masts and after part of the cabin. The Bangor-built *Lewis* stranded nearby, in much the same vulnerable position. Surfmen from Wood End worked valiantly through the day to launch a boat and reach the ves-

sels' stranded sailors, who had taken to the rigging for refuge. But the huge breakers and contrary winds foiled their attempts until late afternoon. By then, all five aboard the *Lewis* and one from the *Mott* had frozen to death. The fortunate survivors had endured 15 numbing hours in the ice-encrusted shrouds.

At Plymouth, more than a dozen craft were injured, either by driving ashore in the harbor or slamming against wharves or other ships. A *Boston Herald* reporter, walking the shore between North Scituate and the Third Cliff, above the North River, encountered seven corpses, three unknown wrecks, and widespread masses of floating wreckage. After the eye-opening experience, he suggested there might be as many as 100 more bodies in the waters between Plymouth and Hull.

Around Boston's inner harbor, at least 25 vessels were driven ashore. The Dorchester and Quincy Bay shallows were literally strewn with damaged and sunken craft. At South Boston, the immense tide lifted the two-masted schooner *Albert H. Harding* over the wharf and dropped it in the Boston Electric Company yard. The schooner *Freddie W. Alton,* which had left Boston on Saturday for Provincetown, was dashed on the beach at Moon Island. The two-master struck rocks off the western side of the island and dragged several hundred yards, stoving her side and becoming a total wreck. Another schooner, *Lizzie Lee*, also went ashore nearby, and several lighters grounded on the adjacent flats.

Between ten and ten-thirty Sunday morning, the Wilson line steamship *Ohio* sailed blindly onto the eastern side of Spectacle Island and stuck fast. Coming in from Hull, England, with 800 tons of freight, Captain William Abbott, the vessel's pilot, claimed the weather was so thick at the time, he "could hardly see across the ship." After days of trying, wreckers finally pulled the steamer free and towed it into dry dock for repairs.

The two-masted schooner *Lizzie Dyas*, carrying a load of Deer Isle granite from Maine, struck near the eastern side of Fort Warren and became a total loss. Another Maine-based schooner, *Virginia*, went ashore nearby; the captain and a crew member perished in the mishap.

North of Boston, scores of broken boats and yachts were numbered among the mounds of debris that choked the shores leading to Cape Ann. Among the fleet of 21 vessels at anchor in Salem harbor, nine dragged onto the surrounding flats or rocky beaches. Three barges, a four-masted schooner, and the revenue cutter *Dallas* were among the lucky vessels which safely rode out the gale in the lower harbor. There was no good fortune a few miles to the northeast, however, where three men from the wrecked schooner *Bessie H. Gross* drowned after the vessel struck the ledges off House Island, Manchester, and went to pieces.

Although no loss of life occurred as a result of the storm in Gloucester harbor, as many as 30 vessels were torn from their moorings and piled up on various parts of the East Gloucester shore. Nine went on at Ten Pound Island; 15 more on the Rocky Neck shore. The refrigerator schooner *J.K. Manning* also stranded, but was afterward pulled off.

At Rockport, eight small fishing craft anchored in the outer harbor became a total loss. Some dragged ashore; the rest sank at their moorings. None was insured. One heroic rescue effort involved saving the crew of the three-masted schooner *Charles E. Schmidt*. The Rockport-based vessel, under the command of Captain Sharp, drifted onto Hale Knowlton's point and firmly wedged on the rocks, with its head to the sea. The crew of seven were taken off the ship Sunday morning, at the very height of the storm, by Captain John Parsons, William Breen, and William Madison, all members of the Davis Neck Life-Saving Station.

The *Ohio* ashore on Spectacle Island in Boston Harbor.

Storm damage was less along the New Hampshire coast, where winds generally topped out at less than 50 miles per hour. Off Portsmouth, however, conditions at the Isles of Shoals were described as "the worst ever known." The steamer *Pinafore* was tossed ashore, a total wreck. Heavy seas heaved thousand-pound granite boulders high onto Appledore Island.

Further north, into Maine, losses were mostly minimal. At Portland and Rockland, several schooners dragged ashore, some having masts or spars snapped, or losing lines and rigging—a fairly common occurrence in heavy weather. Three schooners did go ashore at Fort Point, on the west side of Penobscot Bay, 12 miles upriver from Belfast. *Forest Queen*, of Stonington, became a total loss; *S. C. Tryon*, of Boston, suffered a bad hole in its port quarter; while *Izetta*, of Bangor, suffered only minor damage and was later re-floated. Crews aboard the three vessels were cared for by Capt. Webster, the keeper at nearby Fort Point lighthouse.

The storm-related casualties continued to mount for days afterward, as additional quantities of wreckage washed ashore, providing clues to the fortunes of other vessels, missing or unreported. The most gruesome finds were the lifeless bodies of men, women, and children plucked from the seas or discovered along the beaches, some all but entombed in the ever-shifting dunes. At Cape Cod, occasional, partially decomposed corpses were found as many as six weeks later.

Exactly how great was the overall devastation at sea remains unknown. A week after the storm, the *Boston Globe* reported 155 vessels sunk or destroyed in southern New England waters alone, and as many as 475 lives lost. Later accounts revealed ships and lives taken, from New Jersey to Nova Scotia. An estimated death toll of 500 is no doubt conservative, since many vessels disappeared without a trace, leaving no clue of how many were aboard.

Some idea of the terrors that faced thousands of mariners caught in the great storm may be found in the stories of those who survived their ordeals and told their stories in newspaper accounts. In several instances, the faithfully-kept journals of the various U.S. Life-Saving Service crews give unique, first-hand evidence. From these reports, some idea of the storm's ferocity and the perils of those caught in it is evident, although the full measure of the terror and suffering they experienced can only be imagined.

In the days before ship-to-shore radio, vessels at sea foretold pending weather by carefully observing the types and movements of clouds and noting wind speed and direction. The fact that many mariners sensed stormy conditions were approaching the afternoon of November 26, is evident by the fact so many began scurrying for port into the evening. But when the storm did arrive, it "blew up" so quickly and violently that many were overwhelmed—even ones already close to, or in a normally safe haven.

Despite the great toll, losses would have been significantly higher without the courageous, unselfish work of the members of the U.S. Life-Saving Service. Their daring acts, in the face of perilous conditions and overwhelming danger, saved no fewer than 133 lives throughout New England and recovered untold hundreds of thousands of dollars in vessels and cargo.

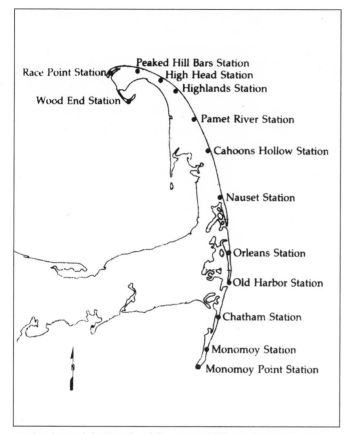

Race Point Station
Peaked Hill Bars Station
High Head Station
Highlands Station
Wood End Station
Pamet River Station
Cahoons Hollow Station
Nauset Station
Orleans Station
Old Harbor Station
Chatham Station
Monomoy Station
Monomoy Point Station

At the time of the *Portland* disaster, 12 life-saving stations were located an average of three to five miles apart along the outer Cape Cod shore, between Provincetown and Monomoy. A thirteenth station, Monomoy Point, was added in 1901.

The noteworthy accomplishments of these crews are rooted in more than a century of similar service along these very shores. They can be traced back to the initial actions of the Massachusetts Humane Society, a volunteer body founded in 1785. The charitable association concentrated its earliest efforts constructing a series of rude, unattended huts along lonely stretches of beach, to shelter shipwrecked souls who had made it safely ashore. Each was equipped with candles, a tinderbox, kindling, and a small amount of non-perishable food. The first Humane House, as it was called, went up in 1789, on Lovell's Island in Boston Harbor. In 1807, the group established the nation's first lifeboat station at Cohasset, about ten miles southeast of Boston Light. From it, crews could launch a specially designed and built, 30-foot dory and go to the aid of distressed vessels. During the next 40 years, MHS erected and maintained a network of 18 similar facilities, mostly shed-type buildings housing lifeboats and rescue gear. It continued operating them into the early 20th century.

Government-sponsored search and rescue operations, which had slowly evolved through the middle years of the nineteenth century, reached Massachusetts during 1872-73, when nine life-saving stations were established—generally at three- to five-mile intervals—along the outer arm of Cape Cod, from Provincetown to Monomoy. They were designated as: Race Point, Peaked Hill Bars, Highland, Pamet River, Cahoons Hollow, Nauset, Orleans, Chatham, and Monomoy. By the close of the century, the network in Massachusetts had expanded to nearly 30 locations—including 12on Cape Cod—with nine more in Rhode Island, three in New Hampshire, and a dozen in Maine.

By the late 1870s, the U.S. Life-Saving Service had become a well-organized, highly efficient, professional organization. In 1878, it was reorganized as an independent agency within the Treasury Department. Most stations operated ten months a year, closing down during June and July, although crews were still on call in the event of an emergency. Individual locations were customarily staffed by a keeper and six to eight surfmen. All were expert at small-boat handling, knowledgeable seamen, physically fit, highly disciplined, and without the slightest fear.

Crews spent extended hours, six days a week, performing repeated training exercises to hone their life-saving skills to the point every technique and movement became instinctive. Prolonged boat drills included launching the station's double-ended surfboat, pulling at the sweeps, and deliberately capsizing and righting the craft. On shore, assembling the beach apparatus, firing the Lyle gun, and working the breeches buoy were equally important tasks to be mastered. Drills were frequently timed, and crews not able to perform routines within the allotted interval risked dismissal from the service.

Routines such as flag signaling, first aid, and artificial respiration also received frequent attention and repetition, while the rigorous maintenance of station equipment was ongoing. Sunset through sunrise meant lookout duty, with surfmen rotating tower watches or going on beach patrol.

When the November 26-27, 1898, storm struck New England, the resident life-saving crews were about their usual business. Their logs report the storm's severity with

Surfmen preparing to leave the Highland Station during the great November gale of 1898.

a matter-of-factness and uncolored brevity that belies the measure of service they performed, but they cannot hide the amazing deeds that so many accomplished in the line of duty.

Among the wrecks the life-savers attended was the Boston pilot boat *Columbia*, which was wrecked off Scituate, on the Boston south shore. Contemporary reports describe the vessel as being "as staunch and seaworthy and ably manned as any craft within the whole radius of the storm." Schooner-rigged and weighing 89 tons, *Columbia* had been built at East Boston in 1895, expressly for pilot service. The 85-foot schooner had been at sea from Boston for about a week before the disaster, delivering pilots to incoming ships. After dropping off William Abbott with the steamer *Ohio* at the outskirts of Massachusetts Bay, Captain Harry Peterson and his four-man crew turned *Columbia* back to port.

Around eight o'clock, Sunday morning, surfman Richard Tobin was walking the south patrol from the North Scituate Life-Saving Station, contending with stinging, sleet-laced snow driven almost horizontally by howling 50 to 70 mile per hour winds. In a later-recorded statement, he related:

> I went down the beach to the key post (the turn-around spot) about three miles from the station. When I started from the station there was much wreckage on the beach... It was blowing so hard that I was obliged to kneel down at times to get my breath. It was a hurricane from the northeast, and snowing so that I could not see any distance offshore. I kept on, and finally I had to take the field back of the beach... I warned a number of people in houses nearby that they had better seek safety elsewhere, as the seas were breaking up against the windows. I helped two families—the women and children—to a safe place in another house...

Tobin started back toward the station around nine-thirty, too soon to be aware of a startling event that occurred along his beat soon after. In fact, its discovery would have to wait until early the next morning. Because of the storm's severity and the flood tides, no further patrols went south from the North Scituate station until after midnight Sunday.

COLUMBIA WRECKED

Boston Pilot Boat Piled Up on the Beach at Scituate.

CREW OF FIVE MEN DROWNED

A *Boston Globe* headline proclaims the *Columbia* tragedy

Then, about one a.m., surfman John Curran, Jr. set out on his rounds. The weather had moderated, but the northwesterly wind still blew a gale and snow continued to fall rather thickly. As Curran reported:

> I walked the regular beat, but of course had to keep back farther on the beach—the sea had made such inroads. At about a quarter of 2 o'clock (Monday morning, November 28), I should judge, I saw the schooner (*Columbia*) right in my line of patrol, lying on the beach (off Cedar Point).

Columbia was high up on the beach, with the mainmast gone and foremast broken off short. The starboard side had been badly stove, split open near the garboard. The planking was badly chafed and broken, showing how se-

The Boston pilot boat *Columbia* hard ashore at Scituate .

FOUR SHORT BLASTS

verely it had ground over the rocks on the way to shore. The stern post had been shattered, and both chains dangled from their respective hawse pipes, each minus its anchor.

Curran returned to the station, where he informed keeper George Brown what had had seen. At 3:20 a.m., Monday, Brown mustered three surfmen and set out toward the wreck. En route, the four came upon a body on the beach, which they carried to a safer place before continuing to the wreck. Although it was still too dark to see that well inside *Columbia's* hull, the life-savers made sure that no one alive was aboard, then waited for daylight. In the first gray light of dawn, they discovered the broken remains of a shorefront cottage canted onto the schooner's deck. The vessel had apparently crashed against it when giant seas drove it to the very height of the beach.

Nobody witnessed the disaster, so no one knows for certain when it took place. The most likely time was during the Sunday forenoon high tide, when the wind was still onshore. A USLSS investigation of the disaster concluded:

> the fact that both the chain cables had parted shows that the vessel had attempted unsuccessfully to weather the storm by means of her anchors. At that time she must have been in dire distress, and there is no telling what straits her crew were then in.

The body the life-savers discovered on the way to the scene proved to be that of Captain Peterson. North Scituate crews remained at the wreck site through Monday. During the day, they spotted three more bodies in the surf, although they were unable to reach them. Over the next 48 hours, farmers gathering rockweed discovered three corpses on shore, although none could positively be identified as any of *Columbia's* crew.

Columbia's wreckage remained on the beach at Scituate into the 1930s, and became a much-visited landmark. Ultimately, town officials decided the decaying remains should be removed and ordered them burned.

Not far from where *Columbia* pounded ashore, legendary keeper Joshua James and the life-savers from the Point Allerton station had to deal with a succession of wrecks which piled up on the south side of Boston Harbor. One was the four-masted schooner *Abel E. Babcock*. The 812-ton vessel was en route from Philadelphia to Boston with a cargo of coal, when it was overtaken by the storm Saturday night. The schooner, commanded by Captain Abel E. Babcock, apparently anchored south of Boston Light, in an attempt to ride out the gale. Unknown to anyone but the eight men aboard, the *Babcock* was unable hold its position against the heavy winds and dragged onto Toddy's Rocks, about a mile north of Hull and halfway between Point Allerton and Fort Warren. The entire crew perished, so no details of the schooner's destruction are known. About five a.m. Sunday, a surfman on the west patrol came upon a large section of the *Babcock's* hull on Windmill Point, but did not locate the bodies of any of the eight victims.

The same morning, keeper James and his crew were able to rescue the seven men aboard the three-masted schooner *Henry R. Tilton*, which was driven onto the Hull shore, a mile and one-half west of the Point Allerton station. According to James, one of the station's lookouts spotted the lumber-laden schooner about three a.m., in distress and directly opposite his position. An hour later, it stranded just west of the station, several hundred yards offshore. The seas were too wild for the life-savers to launch a surfboat, so they fired a shot line aboard the ship and rigged a breeches buoy. In his report, James related some of the dangers involved bringing the stranded crew ashore:

> In the vicinity where this occurred there is a heavy granite sea wall. The men handling the whip line and hawser were obliged to stand on the edge of this wall to keep the line clear of rocks, seaweed, and wreckage. The sea at times would strike the wall, break over, and bury men, beach apparatus, and all, making it very disagreeable and dangerous, also difficult to see when the men got into the breeches buoy.

While the rescue of *Tilton's* crew was still in progress, James and the surfmen learned that a huge barge was ashore less than a mile west of them and had begun breaking up. As the life-savers would learn later, coal barges *No. 1* and *No. 4* had been under tow for Boston, from Baltimore,

The *Henry R. Tilton* after it had been driven ashore at Hull.

Maryland. As the storm increased Saturday night, the two craft, belonging to the Consolidated Coal Company, became unmanageable in the heavy seas and high winds, and the tug bringing the pair along cut the tow lines and abandoned them off Point Allerton.

It was barge *No. 1* that had stranded off the Hull shore, placing Captain Joshua Thomas and four crew members in a highly precarious predicament. The Point Allerton life-savers and members of a neighboring Massachusetts Humane Society crew hastily assembled on the shore opposite the wreck, which was already going to pieces on outlying rocks off Windmill Point. To save themselves, the barge's five-man crew hung on to pieces of wreckage, which the unrelenting waves pushed ever closer to the beach. As soon as the hapless sailors got into the heavy breakers rolling onto the shore, the life-savers tied long lines about their own waists and waded into the surf. Keeper James' unvarnished report explains what transpired:

> The (barge's) house these (crew)men were on broke away from the deck of the barge, and came into the breakers, the men being thrown in a heap, into the surf, near enough for our men to seize them and hold them from going back in the undertow, and as the next sea came they all came up safely together.

According to James, the rescued men were "helpless and chilled through, and it would have been almost murder to try to get them to the station—a mile away—in the severe weather and through the drifts of snow, therefore it was absolutely necessary to go into the nearest house..." Such a place was less than 100 feet away, although it was locked up and unoccupied. Fearing a life-or-death situation, keeper James broke into the dwelling. In his testimony, he stated that once inside the house:

> We found everything needed for the comfort of the men. We made fires, stripped them of their wet clothing, rubbed them and used the comfortables of the house to wrap them in. As soon as they were able they were taken to the station.

The government later paid the property owner for the damage done when the life-savers entered the premises and for all they had appropriated during the stay.

While *No. 1*'s crew survived their harrowing ordeal, not all aboard *No. 4* were as fortunate. Shortly after midnight, the second barge struck the treacherous Toddy's Rocks and promptly pounded to pieces. Before daylight, portions drifted onto Windmill Point, near where wreckage from the schooner *Abel E. Babcock* came up. *No. 4*'s captain and one of the sailors floated ashore by clinging to a section of the deck house. Three others were lost.

It was late Sunday afternoon before Joshua James and the Point Allerton crew returned to the station. Although the winds were still strong and the seas raging, the persistent snowfall occasionally diminished in intensity, and when it did, the visibility improved. During such a lull just before dark, James spotted the masts of a ship on the far side of Little Brewster Island, slightly more than a mile to the north and the site of historic Boston Light. He surmised trouble, but knew his nearly exhausted crew could never reach the exposed location, especially at night and in the face of the wild winds and seas.

James' suspicions were correct. The masts belonged to the schooner *Calvin F. Baker*, en route from Baltimore to Boston with a cargo of coal. Crossing Massachusetts Bay in near zero visibility about three o'clock Sunday morning, the unfortunate vessel—with many of its sails tattered or blown away—stranded on the north side of Little Brewster. The powerful seas pounded the helpless vessel further in, until it fetched up about 75 yards from the rocky shore. Realizing that safety and shelter were available at the nearby lighthouse, the schooner's second mate plunged into the boiling surf and attempted to swim to the beach. He carried with him a line, which he hoped he could fasten somewhere on shore and use to help his shipmates escape. The man drowned in the icy waters before he reached land, and his body was swept away.

Disheartened, the remaining seven climbed into the rigging to avoid the reach of the gigantic breakers sweeping across the ship. When the tide slowly receded Sunday afternoon, the shivering crew found some semblance of shelter beneath a small portion of the forward deck, which had somehow remained intact. Huddling together for any warmth, the marooned sailors remained in their cramped quarters, as one great wave after another engulfed the wreck, drenching their garments before the biting cold further stiffened them into icy boards. After dark, the incoming tide again forced them aloft, into the unprotected

Lifesavers from Hull battling the sea in the successful effort to rescue the crew of the schooner *Calvin S. Baker* at Boston Light.

rigging. Overnight, the ship's steward froze to death and the first mate was swept away when a towering comber collapsed a section of the deck and pitched him into the icy waters.

As it happened, Joshua James had a standing arrangement with the keeper at Boston Light, that if the life-savers' services were ever needed in that vicinity, the keeper would fly a distress signal. Before dawn Monday, James trained his telescope on the light station, and in the graying light he spied the telltale warning flag. Summoning a crew that included four MHS volunteers, he hurried to the inside beach, on the sheltered, south side of the Hull peninsula. Here, the stalwart group launched and pulled a surfboat to Pemberton Landing, just inside Nantasket Gut. James quickly commandeered the tug *Ariel*, which ferried men and surfboat out to Little Brewster. Although the snow had ended and the wind backed into the north-northwest, the seas around the island were still running so high, the tug's captain did not dare go within a quarter of a mile of shore.

The life-savers fell to the task ahead of them, and reaching the wreck was not the least of the challenges. They first had to cross the line of shoals that forms a bar off the island, and the long combers breaking over it made the effort exceedingly dangerous. Pulling with mighty strokes, the crew sent the surfboat headlong into the wild water and shot safely past. From here, it was a comparatively easy approach to the schooner, which lay with its head offshore and the deck mostly gone, except the forward section where the five half-frozen sailors still crouched together, more

Rescued sailors from the schooner *Calvin F. Baker* thawing their frozen feet in pans of snow.

dead than alive. The lifeless body of the steward lay nearby. Strong arms and backs carefully lifted the six bodies into the surfboat and rowed them back to the waiting tug.

Within 90 minutes, the survivors of the *Calvin F. Baker* shipwreck rested at the Point Allerton Life-Saving Station, where compassionate surfmen and a local doctor painstakingly tended to their every need. The life-savers cut away the sailors' frozen boots and garments and bathed their

The steamer *John J. Hill* high and dry at Wollaston Beach

numb, swollen feet with cold water. After four days of rest and nourishment, the rescued mariners had sufficiently revived to leave the station and return to their homes.

When the Point Allerton crew arrived at the station, a concerned Captain Alfred Galiano was awaiting them. Galiano had a message that three men were marooned on Black Rock, beyond the south end of Nantasket Beach and about four miles from the station. A Humane Society crew from Cohasset had recently tried to rescue the trio, but

their surfboat had capsized and they were forced to give up the effort.

By the time keeper James and the Point Allerton life-savers reached the beach opposite where the unlucky victims awaited, more than 100 anxious spectators had gathered to witness the rescue attempt. The U.S. Life-Saving Service's annual report for 1899 describes the ordeal:

> When everything was in readiness Keeper James gave the order to launch, and by a resolute and skillful effort all together the boat shot clear of the beach and proudly mounted the tumbling breakers. This brilliant first victory in the fight evoked the admiration of the onlookers, and at the same time strengthened the arms of the oarsmen who pulled with high hope swiftly over the miles that lay between them and the imperiled men. But on their arrival in the vicinity of Black Rock they found that their eager spirit must not forget discretion to be the better part of valor.
>
>   The sea was still running high, dashing heavily on the rock and flying into the air. To have rushed in at that time might have been bravery, but it would have been madness also, and therefore the keeper...ordered his crew to lie upon the oars. For an hour the boat lay by, idly pitching, tossing to and fro. At last...the breakers left an opening and the boat rushed in. Quickly were the three shivering sailors drawn into it, and, the instant another opening showed, it gallantly dashed out into safer water.

The three rescued men were from *Lucy A. Nickels*, one of

two barges cut adrift off Minot's Light by the tug *Underwriter*. They had reached the ledge by clinging to one of the vessel's masts. The second barge, *Virginia*, foundered offshore. A total of eight crew were losat from both vessels.

At Scituate, the Brant Rock Life-Saving Station crew had its hands full dealing with the multiple, storm-related casualties within its jurisdiction. One was the Boston-based fishing schooner *Mertis H. Perry*, which had been returning from a week-long stay on the fishing grounds 12 miles southeast of Highland Light. The vessel's holds bulged with 15,000 pounds of mixed fish for the Monday market.

Crossing Massachusetts Bay at nine-thirty Saturday evening, the schooner encountered a mix of rain and snow, which appreciably reduced the visibility. By eleven o'clock, the wind had sharply increased and the seas begun building to the extent the skipper, Captain Joshua Pike, decided to wear ship and work offshore. In the rough weather, it was a particularly dangerous maneuver. As Pike attempted to come about, the main gaff broke and the jib split, causing the vessel to lose all headway. Pike then let go both port and starboard anchors, but they were unable to hold the schooner against the already mountainous seas and winds beyond gale force. Sensing no other choice, Pike ordered the masts cut away.

Around two-thirty Sunday morning, *Mertis H. Perry's* port anchor rope parted. Although this put added strain on the starboard chain, it held until shortly after daylight, before it also let go.

Unable to control the ship, Captain Pike decided the best course of action was to head westward, with the wind, and let the heavy gale and huge waves drive it onto the beach. He hoped the schooner would strike high enough on shore that everyone could either save themselves or be rescued. According to Life-Saving Service inspector Captain E.R. Nash, who investigated the incident and reported on it in detail:

The schooner *Mary B. Rogers* ashore at the causeway in the Hough's Neck section of Quincy

She (*Mertis H. Perry*) turned before the storm, which swept her along with the speed of an avalanche, while the crew, to whom the end did not seem far off, clung desperately to the hoops around the stumps of the masts.

The breathless ride did not last long. Within five minutes, *Mertis H. Perry* had reached an area of heavy breakers and almost immediately grounded. As it did, towering seas breached the entire ship, sending dizzying sheets of spray high above the masts. The incoming tide slowly pounded the helpless schooner onward, until the fearful crew could faintly see the fuzzy outline of shore through the swirling snow, no more than a few hundred feet ahead of them.

The frightful ordeal was having its harmful effects on the little schooner's sailors. About eight a.m., crew member Walter Bagnall succumbed to exposure. Captain Pike apparently let helplessness and the fear for the safety of his vessel, the cargo, and remaining crew get the better of him. According to inspector Nash, Pike:

> had evidently become demented from his awful experience, for he abruptly picked up part of a dory which had been smashed in, and, without saying a word, jumped overboard, and was not seen afterwards.

Mertis H. Perry had come ashore at Brant Rock, on the southwest shore of Massachusetts Bay, between Scituate and Duxbury. The forenoon flood tide carried the schooner so high on the sands, the jib boom ultimately projected over the banking that rimmed the top of the beach. Four sailors crawled out on the lengthy spar and dropped onto the bank, but before any more could follow, an immense wave turned the vessel broadside, cutting off the easy means of escape. Those still aboard grabbed a line and flung it to their shipmates on the banking, just as another comber swung the schooner back, with its head to the beach. Momentarily, six more sailors scrambled to safety. The remaining two did not make it; Joseph Veador fell from the boom and drowned, and George Bagnall succumbed from exhaustion and fright while the others were making their escape.

Ten of the 15 comprising *Mertis H. Perry's* crew had survived the harrowing experience. One of them, Charles Forbes, was so far gone, though, he was unable to walk. His mates left him on the bluff while they went searching for shelter and assistance. They soon located the farmhouse of a Mr. Ames, who kindly ushered them in and gave them food and dry clothing. Ames sent two of his farm hands out to bring in Forbes, but by the time they arrived at the shore, the poor sailor had passed away.

That afternoon, surfmen from the Brant Rock station removed William and George Bagnall's bodies from the schooner and took them, together with that of Charles Forbes, to an undertaker at Marshfield. The body of one of the drowned victims was found the next day near the entrance to Green Harbor, and Captain Pike's later washed ashore on Gurnet Beach.

The life-savers might ordinarily have located *Mertis H. Perry* as soon as it reached shore, since the ship grounded only two miles north of the Brant Rock station. But the extraordinary tide had so badly flooded the surrounding countryside, it made shore patrols difficult in places and downright impossible in others. Sunday morning's wild seas cut through the bank a mile north of the station, preventing surfmen from checking the beach beyond that point. The situation was little better to the south. The same storm surge breached the Marshfield dike, at the head of Green Harbor, making further progress in that direction also unachievable.

Along the outer shores of Cape Cod, life-savers from Race Point to Monomoy faced some of the worst conditions the great November 1898 gale delivered. One of the many disasters these crews encountered was the wreck of the schooner *Albert L. Butler*. The 344-ton vessel had been trying to reach Boston harbor from Jamaica, with a capacity cargo of logwood.

The *Butler's* skipper, Captain Frank A. Leland, had endured a difficult passage, sailing against strong headwinds most of the way north along the Atlantic coast. Saturday evening, November 26, Leland estimated he was some 40 miles east-southeast of Highland Light, on Cape Cod's northeast curl, and was enjoying a light southeasterly breeze, which would help him speed the final leg of the trip. By midnight, he reckoned he had run north by northwest another 28 miles, but in the meantime, the wind had backed and become a northeasterly gale. Fearing the approaching lee shore, he hauled off under short sail, until he supposed he had run another 20 miles to the north. At that point, he hove to and, according to his calculations, "made a dead drift of about 15 miles."

Shortly after daylight, Sunday, Captain Leland feared he was approaching the Cape Cod beaches and wore ship under bare poles. In his words, "The sea was frightful, the biggest I ever saw, and the gale swept us at its mercy." At seven a.m., a tremendous sea engulfed the ship, scattering the deck load of lumber and driving portions of it through the sails. The hurtling logs acted as out-of-control battering rams, carrying away booms and gaffs, smashing in doors and hatches, and leaving the ship a badly battered hulk.

Now fully at the mercy of the raging storm, *Albert L. Butler* continued to drift closer to the northern tip of Cape Cod. About ten a.m., the forefoot got into breakers in shoal water, and the schooner swung broadside and landed high on the beach.

As the *Butler* was approaching the shore, surfman B.F. Henderson from the Peaked Hill Bars Life-Saving Station had reached the eastern end of his patrol, when he met Benjamin Kelley, from High Head, near the halfway house between the two outposts. Although anxious for shelter from the powerful storm, neither one dared enter the little shack as they normally would, because the unusually high surf was breaking over it. The pair talked briefly and agreed this was the worst weather they had ever experienced. They decided to rest a few moments on the dune at the top of the beach, while they continued to scan the storm-tossed seas for signs of vessels in distress.

The two life-savers were about to part company and head back to their respective stations, when they spotted the defenseless hulk of *Albert L. Butler* broadside in the seas, moments before it grounded in the surf. Henderson and Kelley knew what they must do. Moving as quickly as they could through the drifted sand and snow, the two life-savers ran to alert their respective crews.

Surfman Henderson realized the wreck lay within the limits of his station and his fellow crew members would be responsible for a rescue attempt. He covered the 3 1/2-mile distance to the station in 30 minutes, despite a smothering wind that swept sleet and fine grains of sand in lofty swirls and stung his face. Benjamin Kelley was not much longer getting back to High Head. Hearing Henderson's news, Peaked Hill Bars keeper William W. Cook ordered the light beach cart and gear run out and hitched to a horse. He and the crew dressed quickly and started for the wreck.

Forcing the big-wheeled beach cart through the deep, soft sand at the fastest possible pace, the all-but-breathless crew arrived opposite the stranded schooner just after eleven a.m., shortly before a contingent from High Head appeared. Overhead, flashes of lightning and bursts of thunder added to the unfolding drama at hand. As they surveyed the scene, the life-savers spotted a man lying on the banking above the beach. Someone had apparently

managed to get ashore and survive.

The beached *Albert L. Butler* lay about 150 feet from the beach. Placing a Lyle gun on the bank for greater elevation, keeper Cook landed a line aboard the ship, between the main and mizzen masts. But, for whatever reason, the sailors on deck made no attempt to snare or make it fast. Cook and the crew tried to shout across instructions, but the roaring wind and crashing surf made voice communication impossible. Cook fired again, this time dropping the light line squarely across the schooner's deck, almost within arm's length of one of the sailors. The fellow seized it, hauled the whip line aboard, and fastened the tail block in the mizzen rigging. But rather than wait for the heavier hawser and breeches buoy to be sent over, the man started

The *Albert L. Butler*.

to come ashore holding the whip line. As he did, the slender line sagged and dropped him into the tumultuous surf. The life-savers scrambled to haul the poor sailor through the breakers and managed to draw him up onto the shore before he drowned.

Soon after the first rescue, the *Butler's* mizzenmast let go and crashed forward, going by the board and fouling the whip line. Thinking the schooner was going to pieces around them, two of the sailors grabbed the whip line and tried to reach shore as their shipmate had attempted. The life-savers tried to signal the pair to wait until they could send out a heavier line, but their appeal went unheeded. The pair grabbed the whip line, but when the surfmen began hauling, the snarl of ropes at the other end prevented it from running through the tail block. At that very moment, according to keeper Cook:

> ...a big sea, I should say twenty feet high, rolled in and buried the vessel, men, and everything. I had hold of the whip line, and could feel when the sailors lost their grasp. They were washed off, and that was the last we knew of them.

While the crew were pondering the unfortunate moment, they heard a cry from under the bank below them. Peering over the edge, they saw a man trying to climb up. His discovery meant three of *Butler's* crew were safe, although all were suffering from exposure and minor injuries, and needed shelter and attention. Gathering them about him, Cook questioned them about the ship and their mates, but each one said no one else was still aboard. Cook then sent the trio on to the Peaked Hill Bars station, in charge of two of the High Head patrol. Before he de-

parted, he ordered two of his own crew—surfmen Fish and Kelley—to watch the wreck and get aboard as soon as the tide went down. Then he and the others went back to the station.

By two o'clock, the tide had receded enough that the *Butler's* hull was beginning to emerge from the wash. Awaiting their chance to climb aboard, life-savers Fish and Kelley were rather astonished when two more sailors suddenly jumped from the schooner, onto the beach. The pair had retreated to the cabin when the schooner struck and remained there with no knowledge of their shipmates' situation. The surfmen escorted the pair to the Peaked Hill Bars station, where they were reunited with the three other survivors.

The five shipwrecked mariners remained at the life-saving station for two days, when they were well enough to leave. The wrecked *Albert L. Butler* and its cargo were declared a total loss.

Near sundown Saturday, November 26, a pair of schooners moored in Menemsha Bight, a once-favorite anchorage for sailing craft passing through Vineyard Sound. The spot is approximately two miles east of the Gay Head Life-Saving Station, overlooking the western end of Martha's Vineyard, south of Cape Cod. The vessels' masters, wary of a rising southeasterly wind, apparently viewed the broad bay as good shelter until the weather turned more favorable. One was the three-master *Amelia G. Ireland*, of New York, bound from Bayonne, New Jersey, to Boston, with a cargo of oil in iron tanks. The other, the Portland, Maine-based *Clara Leavitt*, was heading home from Perth Amboy, New Jersey, with a consignment of molding clay. The anchorage was frequently used, especially during southeast storms, and the arrival of the two ships caused no special notice.

As the evening wore on, the wind continued to strengthen. By eight o'clock, it had backed into the east-northeast and drove a mix of snow and rain before it as it thundered down Vineyard Sound. From the Gay Head station, the night patrols were starting on their customary rounds, cautioned to be particularly alert because of the deteriorating conditions. Shortly after ten p.m., surfman Francis Manning, walking the easterly beat, spotted a flash of light in the vicinity of Dogfish Bar, a shoal on the western side of Menemsha Bight. The momentary gleam was enough to reveal the outline of a vessel he sensed was ashore. Manning lighted one red Coston signal, then another, to alert anyone aboard he had sighted the vessel. Planting the beacons in the sand, he hustled the mile and one-half back to the station, to alert keeper N.C. Hayman and his mates.

Hayman and the station's entire crew, except for patrolman Cahoon—still out on the south patrol—promptly loaded a surfboat aboard a wagon and hauled the weighty vehicle along the sandy shore, toward the bight. Hoping to make better progress away from the soft surface, they detoured to higher ground through a cut in the bank. The earth was harder here, but the rugged terrain and the inky blackness made the going ever so slow. In frustration, keeper Hayman sent surfman Ben Altaquin to a nearby farmhouse to ask the owner, Simon Devine, if they could borrow a yoke of oxen to pull the cart. Devine was gladly willing, and by midnight, oxen, cart, and crew had reached the shore, opposite the wreck.

From here, the life-savers could make out the lights of the schooner, roughly a third of a mile away. It was the 284-ton *Amelia G. Ireland*, which had dragged its anchors in the intensifying gale and grounded on the shoals. The surfmen prepared to launch the boat, but at this spot, the heavy wind was blowing directly onshore and beat back their repeated efforts, even though they waded into the surf up to their armpits to guide it on its way. In the midst of their efforts, the surfmen watched with helplessness as a second, larger vessel crashed against the bar, less than 100 yards from where the *Ireland* lay.

By two a.m. Sunday, keeper Hayman reluctantly gave up trying to use the surfboat in the rescue attempt. He sent some of the crew back to the station for the beach apparatus—Lyle gun, powder, projectiles, lines, and breeches buoy, etc. He had little faith he could reach the wrecks at such a distance to windward, but he would try every possibility, no matter how slim.

Meanwhile, the storm continued to grow stronger. The second schooner, *Clara Leavitt*, had struck a particularly exposed spot and began to break up almost at once. Within 20 minutes, seas had destroyed the deckhouse, forcing the seven sailors into the rigging. Soon, wreckage from the ship began piling up on the beach. Hayman and the crew scattered along the shore, watching for anyone from either vessel who might also float in. While they were glancing over the waves, a mighty gust of wind caught the surfboat and tossed it more than 200 feet across the beach, where it landed in a small pond below the bank.

About dawn, those who had gone to the boathouse for the beach apparatus returned from the difficult, six-mile journey. In the first gray streaks of daylight, the life-savers could see men in *Amelia G. Ireland's* rigging. But there was no sign of the other vessel—*Clara Leavitt*. Unknown to those ashore, the 455-ton schooner had been beaten to pieces within an hour of stranding. Shortly after the crew had taken refuge aloft, the schooner's three masts fell and six sailors were drowned. The seventh, seaman Philo J. Sparrow, went overboard with the foremast. He managed to grab a floating stanchion and hold on until the huge waves tossed him up on shore. Seeing no signs of the life-saving crew—nor they of him—Sparrow crawled on his hands and knees across the beach. Above the bank, he found a road which he followed until he reached a house. He roused the owner, Charles H. Ryan, who took the exhausted fellow in, fed, and cared for him.

Keeper Hayman spent the daylight hours Sunday trying to reach the stranded men aboard the schooner *Amelia G. Ireland*. He tried repeatedly with the Lyle gun to heave a projectile and line to the ship, eventually using powder charges well beyond what regulations permitted. But the contrary winds continued too strong and prevented his success.

By late afternoon, keeper Hayman had become discouraged and gave up the effort. His crew had been on duty for 18 straight hours, and they were cold, hungry, and physically spent. He knew they would need some rest if they were to endure further efforts to reach the schooner. Fortunately, the vessel showed no signs of breaking up, as *Clara Leavitt* had done. Leaving two fishermen on the beach to keep a fire burning and maintain a lookout, Hayman and the surfmen hiked back to the station to change clothes, get something to eat, and take a short nap before returning to the beach.

The Gay Head life-savers' respite was a brief one. Before midnight Sunday, they were back at the beach, ready for a further attempt to launch the surfboat. Hauling the craft to a slightly less exposed spot, west of where they had tried before, eight of the crew eventually shot clear of the beach. Pulling out to the reef, the heartened rescuers worked their way through a tangled mass of spars, planks, sails, and rigging, directly alongside the wrecked schooner. Within minutes, they had plucked six grateful sailors from *Ireland's* rolling deck. A seventh had frozen in the rigging before help arrived. It proved to be the ship's mate, who was later buried in the cemetery at Gay Head.

The seven survivors—one of seven of *Leavitt's* crew; six of seven from *Amelia G. Ireland*—were sheltered at the Gay Head station for four days before being taken to New Bedford aboard the revenue cutter *Dexter*. The schooner and its cargo, together valued at $13,000, were a total loss.

The Storm's Effects Ashore

As the great gale of November 1898 swept up the Atlantic coast, it spawned some of the wildest weather ever seen in an autumn storm. Creating in places the combined effects of blizzard, hurricane, and flood, it literally paralyzed dozens of communities from New York to Maine. Some did not fully recover for days after its departure.

In New York City, conditions were reportedly the worst since the landmark "Blizzard of '88." There, the storm began Saturday noon as "soft sleety snow" and continued until ten o'clock Sunday morning. Driven by howling 50- to 65-mile-per-hour winds, the 10 inches of freshly fallen powder piled into mammoth drifts which reappeared nearly as quickly as street crews removed them. The powerful gales forced the almost total suspension of steam and electric car service in and around town. The tracks of the New York, New Haven & Hartford and Long Island railroads disappeared under a sea of white, covered in places to a depth of 16 feet. Outside the city, the situation was much the same. Setauket, on the south shore of Long Island Sound, received a 16-inch accumulation, and amounts of well over a foot were common in neighboring towns and villages.

It was north of the sound where the belt of extreme snowfall occurred. Southern and central Connecticut were buried under an average of two to three feet of wind-blown snow, which slowed, then stopped the majority of rail travel. Middletown was the big winner, receiving 39.0 inches, while surrounding communities measured almost as much—Bridgeport, 33.2; Hartford, 29.5; New London, 31.2; and Waterbury, 27.0. Gales here were strong, but not overwhelming, generally topping out in the 45- to 55-mile-per-hour range. The more modest velocities, coupled with the dry texture of the snow, kept property damage minor.

In Rhode Island, near blizzard conditions left a nearly two-foot blanket of cover. Bristol saw 21 inches; Providence and Kingston, 20 each; and Pawtucket, 18. Near Kingston, drifts of 25 feet stalled trains on the New York, New Haven & Hartford line for 30 hours. An express from Boston to Providence got stuck in an immense bank only a mile and a half from its destination. Workers took 12 hours to shovel and plow the tracks enough for the beleaguered engine to finally crawl into town.

On Block Island, ten miles off the Rhode Island coast, it was the wind rather than the snow which caused the biggest problems. Sunday morning's blasts officially reached 90 miles per hour. Later gusts were estimated as high as 110 m.p.h.

Whipped to a frenzy by the extreme velocities, gigantic seas made a clean sweep over every breakwater on the island. Angry waves breached Ocean Avenue, sending water to the front steps of several of the great hotels and destroying the newly laid macadam roadway. The hotels themselves sustained significant wind damage. The Ocean View, Woonsocket, Eureka, Spring House, Highland House, and Hygeia suffered most—cupolas were torn away, piazzas smashed, and clapboards and blinds torn off. Elsewhere, the Block Island Street Railway Company's brand new car barn collapsed in pieces.

Cape Cod, directly in the storm's path, suffered the full effects of both wind and water. William Swan, an Associated Press reporter from Boston, toured the peninsula two days after the blow and filed the following report:

> I was on Cape Cod Tuesday after the storm and talked with may of the life-savers and others who were out in the blow, and they all seemed to agree that nothing so severe has ever been experienced in that part of the country.
>
> The heft of the storm seems to have been about the time or shortly after the center passed over the Cape, which is generally agreed to have been about 9:30 on Sunday morning. The sky at that time over the stretch between Chatham and Barnstable cleared off entirely and the wind died out. Fifteen minutes after, it was blowing hard from the north, and it was at this time that the gale wrought the greatest destruction among the trees from Yarmouth to Middleboro. In his respect, Sandwich seems to have suffered the most, for not only did the silver oaks, as they are called, go down, but great elms in the town of Sandwich were blown across the streets, and it was a day or two before the main street was passable.
>
> I could not find that the storm center was seen at Provincetown or anywhere north of Eastham, but from the direction of the wind it seems probable that the storm took a diagonal course over the Cape.

From one end of the Cape to the other, the stories of devastation were much the same. Nine wharves along the Provincetown waterfront blew down, as did 21 buildings

Clearing a fallen tree after it had blocked the rail line.

around town. The wind at Woods Hole reached 78 miles an hour, eclipsing the all-time record of 72 m.p.h. The bulk of the precipitation in most places fell as rain, at least until late in the storm. Hyannis managed seven inches of wet snow, although lesser amounts were noted further east.

Torrential rains and flooding tides undermined sections of railroad tracks at several points, and powerful winds flattened poles and tore down miles of wires, effectively cutting off communication with the rest of the world until Tuesday. Lengthy washouts occurred near North Truro, Barnstable, and East Sandwich.

Along the Boston south shore, from Plymouth to Hull, damage to oceanfront property was all but indescribable. Onshore winds along the western rim of Massachusetts Bay pushed a

Damage on Provincetown's Commercial Street after the gale.

Bucking the storm in downtown Boston.

massive storm surge across the coast, overflowing and reconfiguring it as none of the oldest inhabitants could ever recall. Hundreds of shore-facing homes and cottages, together with hotels and other commercial properties, were literally splintered by Sunday forenoon's record tide, which was punctuated by long, rolling combers and wildly crashing surf. Many structures which weren't destroyed outright were lifted from their foundations by the rising waters and unceremoniously deposited elsewhere—in twisted or broken heaps.

Of the 14 cottages formerly lining the long sandy spit that forms Plymouth Beach, only two were still standing when the angry seas receded. Water Street, along the inner harborfront, lived up to its name when the advancing waters submerged the length of it. Immediately south, the bridge crossing the mouth of Town Brook was floated from its foundation and carried upstream. Damaging winds downed several large trees around town and blew the belfry of the Town Square Church nearly 600 feet. Three buildings at George Jackson's lumber yard "were converted into matchwood," according to an eyewitness account. The Plymouth Yacht Club's house was moved several feet before being tipped over on its side.

The relentless gales also lifted a monster tide far above normal in Scituate Harbor, where the wharves along Front Street went three feet under water. A surfman from the North Scituate Life-Saving Station was forced to climb a large tree and remain several hours when the rapidly rising seas cut off his route of escape during the morning beach patrol. His mates fared no better. The unanticipated tidal surge flooded the first floor of the life-saving station, and Captain George H. Brown and the crew had to seek refuge in the second story, not knowing from one moment to the next whether the structure would hold together or remain put. Before subsiding, turbulent seas carried away the runway in front of the wagon room door and left the lawn surrounding the building buried beneath four feet of sand and stones.

In Scituate's Sand Hills neighborhood, more than 60 cottages were either damaged or destroyed, including Station No. 27 of the Massachusetts Humane Society, which floated from its foundation in one direction, while the surfboat went another.

At Cohasset, the storm proved more destructive to property than any since the great tempest of April 1851, which toppled the skeletal tower supporting the original Minot's Ledge Light. Waves carried the fashionable yacht *Zulu* ashore and deposited it high and dry in the middle of the main street.

In Hingham Cove, the devastation was widespread. At high tide, all the roads from Cottage Street to the steamboat wharf disappeared under two feet of water. Whitney's lumber wharf was swept clean, and the deadly, floating debris destroyed eight rowboats and the sloop yacht *Kathleen.* The steamboat wharf itself was lifted from its pilings and and carried several feet, as were the adjacent bathhouses. Six hundred feet of the sea wall along Summer Street washed away. The fast-flowing flood also swept through the street railway car barn, undermining the tracks and dumping a number of the cars in a ditch.

Near or actual hurricane force winds took down dozens of the elm trees for which the town of Hull was famous and felled hundred of telephone and telegraph poles. Many streets were entirely blocked by the snarled debris. And even where public ways might otherwise have been passable, the interminable seas encroached. Officials suspended service on the Nantasket Line of the New York, New Haven & Hartford Railroad because the foundation supporting the rails and ties either washed out numerous sections, or the tracks themselves were bent into grotesque shapes by the ocean's incredible power.

A *Boston Globe* reporter trying to describe the damage along Nantasket Beach could only remark that:

standing by the Atlantic House and looking up the beach, everything is seen to be destroyed as far as the eye can reach...excepting the chutes and the Hotel Nantasket. The Rockland Cafe is gone and...many of the smaller hotels along the beach will be found to be wrecked, if not demolished, while the smaller structures are simply wiped out.

In Boston proper, snow fell from 7:37 Saturday evening through 1:45 Sunday afternoon—piling up a total of 10 inches, before an additional two more filtered down be-

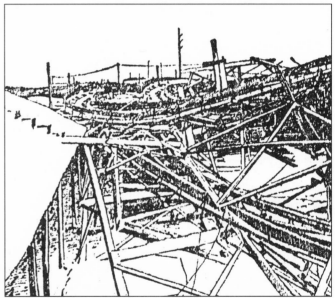

A section of Nantasket's demolished snow-covered rollercoaster.

Destruction at Nantasket Beach.

"The trolley is stuck!"

tween four and ten p.m. It was the city's greatest-ever single storm total for November and the second heaviest accumulation for any month during the previous 14 years. The accompanying winds became particularly intense Sunday forenoon, gusting to 72 miles per hour and creating huge drifts which clogged streets and rail lines, stalling most public transportation. The Boston Elevated Railway Company employed 1,500 men and 230 plows and scrapers to clear the tracks and restore service on its lines.

Tides rose over most waterfront wharves, destroying stockpiles of merchandise in adjoining warehouses. Cap-

tain Bragdon of the harbor police found it difficult to assess the widespread damage. Talking with a *Boston Herald* reporter, he claimed he had never seen such a disastrous high tide in his 30 years on the force. In his words:

> We encountered one of the heaviest seas that I have ever witnessed. I never saw anything like it in my life. There are coasting vessels ashore in a dozen different places, and it will be necessary to lighten these vessels or dig a channel to them.
> Along the waterfront the high tide was something extraordinary. The water came up as far as Commercial Street. The combination of the high tide and the northeast storm did at least $500,000 damage.

If anything, Bragdon's reaction may have underestimated the awful toll. The storm wholly or partially wrecked 30 vessels within the harbor and claimed 40 lives.

North of the city, Revere's storm-swept shoreline took on what the *Boston Herald* termed "a strange, wild, and woebegone appearance," its line of oceanfront properties reduced to a line of "wreck and ruin."

At Salem, the 20 inches of badly-drifted snow that coated the landscape were of secondary concern to the dozens of large trees which came crashing down, severing power and phone lines, bringing hundreds of poles with them and cutting off communication and travel. The furious winds seemed able to move anything, regardless of size or weight. It blew yachts in Frisbie's yard off their cradles and caved in a 175-foot-long shed on Derby's wharf.

Around Gloucester, the mighty gusts collapsed the new brick

and iron Gloucester Street Railway storage house, demolishing 17 new and four older streetcars. Most of the overhead trolley lines around town were torn down, as well, and the tall chimney at the power house was toppled, causing an estimated $20,000 loss. At Pigeon Cove, tides destroyed the Massachusetts Humane Society's shelter, and several hundred tons of coal washed into the sea.

In Newburyport, the northeaster blew out the windows in hundreds of houses, where residents "were much distressed lest their homes themselves would be overturned."

Interior sections of eastern and central Massachusetts were staggered by the remarkable storm, as well. At Worcester, the snow began around six p.m. Saturday and continued at the rate of more than an inch an hour, piling up two feet on the level by mid-afternoon Sunday. Street railway crews eventually abandoned several cars on the local lines, returning on Monday to dig them out and restore service. On Front Street, drifts 12 feet high reached the tops of storefront windows.

Twenty miles to the north, a record-breaking three to four feet of snow bombarded the Fitchburg area, where a correspondent for the *Boston Herald* wrote, "The snowfall of the March blizzard of '88 has been outdone in a shorter time...Stores are concealed from view and everything is demoralized."

South-central sections of the state also took it on the chin from the heavy snow. Intown Springfield counted 21.0 inches, while nearby Monson measured 28.5. Winds in both locales banked up great drifts, but caused only inconsequential damage.

Throughout New Hampshire and Maine, where November snows are more common, the storm was severe, but proved little more than an inconvenience for most people. Concord, New Hampshire, received 18 inches of snow—a new record for No-

vember storms—while Exeter saw 12.

Snowfall totals in the Pine Tree State were heaviest near the New Hampshire border and in the foothills of the western mountains. Cornish reported 21.5 inches and Farmington 20.5. Nearer the coast, amounts were in the order of a foot or more. Gardiner checked in with 14.0; Belfast, 12.0; and Calais, 13.0. The 14 inches dumped on Portland blew around enough to "hide the store windows" on Congress Street, according to the *Evening Express.*

Winds across the state remained generally less than 50 miles an hour, except in exposed coastal locations, where light keepers at Boon Island and Monhegan reported extreme gusts approaching hurricane strength.

While not as devastating over land as at sea, the November 1898 gale still ranks as one of New England's most impressive autumn storms.

Demolished cottages at Revere Beach.

The Portland Sinking:
More Questions Than Answers

Audrey Whitten Thompson   Letitia A. Whitten

As New England's most disastrous maritime tragedy, the sinking of the steamer *Portland* has had a lasting impact on generations of families throughout the six-state area. The untimely deaths of the nearly 200 people aboard touched and altered the lives of thousands of relatives and loved ones, besides generations of their descendants. In greater Portland, home to roughly half the crew and more than one-third of the passengers, the calamity created a deep sense of loss which, for some, would never completely heal.

John C. Whitten of Milbridge, Maine, a watchman on the *Portland*, went down with the ship, leaving Letitia A. Whitten, his widow, to raise three sons and a daughter. The family was so impoverished following the death of John that Letitia put her six-year old daughter up for adoption. The young girl was taken in by Dr. John Thompson, a prominent Portland physician.

Portland's black community suffered the most. With a handful of exceptions, the 30-plus crew members residing there were African Americans. Their ranks included: steward Alonzo V. Matthews, second steward Eben Heusten, first cook Stephen Howard, acting second cook John Jones, cabinman William A. Hemmingway, saloon watchmen Arthur C. Johnston and Theodore Mundrucen, porter Henry G. Allen, and forward cabin watch Griffin Reed. Several were married and left behind grieving wives, husbands, children, or other family members highly dependent on them.

W. Jeffrey Bolster's book *Black Jacks* points out why a tragedy such as the *Portland* sinking would have this drastic an effect:

> Black sailors in Portland, Maine, had a degree of residential and occupational stability atypical (of those) in larger cities such as Baltimore or New York. Of thirty-three black seamen listed in the city directory in 1830, nine lived there sixteen years later, most shipping out, and many at the same addresses.

Alonzo V. Mathews
Steward

Lee Foreman
Saloonman

Peter Rochibeau
Baggage Master

Stephen Howard
First Cook

Thomas H. Pernell
Fireman

William A. Hemmenway
Cabinman

William Lattimer
Head Saloonman

Michael Menott
Saloonman

A selection of newspaper portraits of Portland *crew members*

The fact that black mariners had families ashore made them more likely than footloose white deckhands to ship out of a home port regularly and keep returning there. It also meant that maritime tragedies struck directly at the black community struggling for stability and respectability on shore... Black sailors were older than their white shipmates; more rooted in their home ports; more likely to be married; more likely to persist in going to sea; and more likely to define themselves with dignity as respectable men, because seafaring enabled at least some of them to provide for their families.

On Sunday, December 4, most Portland churchgoers attended services where special sermons were preached or memorial observances held in connection with the loss of the steamer. At the Abyssinian Church, Reverend Theobold Smyth lead a solemn liturgy in memory of 19 of its black members, including two trustees, who perished when the steamship sank. First Parish church pastor John Carroll Perkins eulogized the life of Miss Emily Cobb, another passenger, who was to have sung for the congregation that day. Extended reference to the occurrence was also made at St. Stephens Episcopal, Chestnut Methodist, First Universalist, and Second Parish churches, among others.

For too many, regardless of their beliefs, the hurt was all the more painful because so little could ever be learned about *Portland's* last hours. The mystery of the steamship's disappearance left haunting questions that begged answers: Why did Captain Blanchard sail? How did *Portland* meet its fate? When and where was the steamer forced from its intended route? Was the ship suddenly overwhelmed, so that it foundered quickly; or was it somehow disabled and compelled to drift helplessly, battered unmercifully by gigantic seas before it ultimately sank? Might it have collided with another vessel? What became of the more than 150 bodies that were never found? How many were entombed in the bowels of the ship, or buried in the shifting sands along and above the Cape Cod beaches? How many others drifted away, lost forever?

The last uncertainties were particularly disconcerting to those closest to the victims never located. The fact that fewer than one-fourth of all bodies was ever recovered made final closure of the tragedy extra difficult for hundreds of sorrowing friends and relations.

Captain Hollis Blanchard's reason for taking Portland to sea that night must remain one of conjecture, since it was a decision he apparently shared with no one prior to sailing. There is nothing to indicate he was at all reckless; quite to the contrary. According to longtime Boston weathercaster E.B. Rideout, Blanchard had previously confided to staff at the Weather Bureau office in Boston that his superiors had told him he was "...too cautious, in view of the fact that the alternate and competitive route would be by rail, (and) he would henceforth sail on their orders."

The steamer *Portland* painted by Antonio Nicolo Gasparo Jacobsen.

Captain Blanchard came from a seafaring family. His father, grandfather, uncles, cousins, and two brothers were all ship captains. Young Hollis learned seamanship in the merchant marine and began steamboating during the mid-1880s. He compiled a record of more than eight years of exemplary service with the Portland Steamship Company, serving as first pilot on both *Bay State* and *Portland* before succeeding former *Portland* skipper Captain William Snowman on the latter's death.

Hollis H. Blanchard

Surviving accounts of Blan-chard's inclinations in the hours prior to *Portland's* final trip are fragmentary, at best, and only hint at how they may have affected his judgment whether to go. He did have conversations about the impending weather with friends, fellow mariners, and some of the steamer's passengers, although there's no clear evidence that anyone's comments actually swayed his thoughts. In the days and years since the tragedy, numerous anecdotal accounts of these exchanges have surfaced, and they continue to fuel the speculation.

Boston and Portland newspapers reported that during Saturday afternoon, *Bay State's* skipper, Alexander Dennison, telephoned Captain Blanchard from Portland.

The two exchanged remarks about the wisdom of sailing, based on the special weather advisory issued that forenoon. According to the *Portland Daily Advertiser*, "Captain Dennison said it looked black, (in Portland) and he should wait until 8 or 9 o'clock." Blanchard, on the other hand, told Dennison he "wanted to spend Sunday in Portland."

On the Wednesday following the disaster, the *Boston Evening Transcript* ran a "rumor has it" item which the paper claimed might have influenced Captain Blanchard's thinking. It stated that Blanchard had recently anticipated getting command of *Portland's* sister ship, *Bay State*, but was disappointed when the company chose the younger, less experienced Alexander Dennison instead. According to the story, when Blanchard learned that Dennison intended to keep *Bay State* in port that Saturday night, he determined he would demonstrate his superior seamanship and "proudly steam into Portland harbor Sunday morning and show...that he could take his ship through any storm without fear."

Years afterward, Mrs. Carrie Courtney, a member of the Lewiston (Maine) High School class of 1881, affirmed that she boarded *Portland* as a passenger Saturday evening, but changed her mind shortly before sailing time, deciding to take the train instead. She maintained that while aboard she spoke with Captain Blanchard, who showed her a watch he had bought for his daughter and said he was looking forward to giving her a "coming out party" when he got home.

A youthful Salvation Army lass claimed to have encountered Captain Blanchard having supper with another man in a Boston waterfront restaurant not long before the captain returned to the wharf, prior to sailing time. The young lady, whose first name was Ethel, was peddling copies of the Army's weekly *War Cry* newspaper along the waterfront. Recalling the incident many years later, she stated that she sold a copy to the pair and "while making change, I overheard a few words of their conversation; it was about the weather and the forthcoming night, about which they expressed some anxiety."

Captain C.H. Leighton, of Rockland, Maine, chatted with Captain Blanchard aboard *Portland* about an hour before the ship sailed. In a front-page story in the *Portland Evening Express,* Leighton stated he had intended to sail on the steamer that night, but changed his mind in the face of the ominous weather forecast. The *Express* reported the following conversation between the two:

> "Captain Blanchard, are you going to sail on such a night as this?"
> "I think I shall, Captain Leighton," he replied.
> "By George, Captain," said Captain Leighton, "I don't think this is a fit night to leave port."
> "I don't know about that," said Captain Blanchard, "we may have a good chance."
> ...on parting with Captain Blanchard, (Leighton) said: "I am going back to my house in Chelsea."

Steamship Company general manager John F. Liscomb called India Wharf from Portland shortly before five-thirty Saturday afternoon. Speaking with Charles F. Williams, the firm's Boston agent, Liscomb left word that because of the threatening weather, *Bay State* would not sail for Boston that evening. He also asked Williams if he could talk with Captain Blanchard. Williams replied that Blanchard wasn't there, but would return soon. According to Williams' statement to the press the following week, Liscomb directed him to tell Blanchard to hold *Portland* at the wharf until 9:00 p.m., and if conditions were worsening, to cancel the trip. Liscomb then left the steamship office and caught the 6:00 p.m. train to Boston, so he could attend the funeral of Captain Charles Deering, late skipper of *Bay State*. Deering, 73, had passed away Thanksgiving night at his home in East Boston.

Moments later, Blanchard returned to the office and learned that Liscomb had called. According to accounts in the Boston papers *Herald* and *Globe*, Blanchard ostensibly remarked that *Portland* would sail on schedule—at 7:00 p.m. The initial news stories were harsh on Blanchard for this, citing his decision as "...contrary to the direct orders of Mr. Liscomb" and "...a sad error of judgment...that he should leave in the face of explicit directions to the contrary." *The Washington Evening Star* was particularly critical. In a November 30 editorial, it chided:

> The *Portland's* captain ignored the official warning...and the direct orders of his superior to keep in port. He carried with him to death over 100 people, who had no knowledge, presumably, of the desperate chances which he was taking. This tragedy serves to suggest that perhaps there may be some more positive method of preventing disasters in the face of solemn warning that dan-

ger is at hand. The traveling public ought to have some safeguard against this chance of death. A foolhardy commander should not be permitted to carry out to meet the hurricane his crew and passengers who rely upon his judgment...It may perhaps be possible for the States to go farther and take steps to actually prevent the sailing of vessels under such circumstances.

The papers' condemnations were later challenged by Captain Blanchard's granddaughter. In an interview with the late author Edward Rowe Snow, Miss Grace Blanchard claimed that her father (Captain Blanchard's son, who lived in Boston) was also aboard *Portland* shortly before sailing time and asked his father if it were really necessary for him to go. In her words, the captain responded, "I have my orders to sail, and I am going!"

And, in fact, during the days and weeks that followed, most newspaper critics softened their stance, eventually upholding the growing public opinion in favor of Captain Blanchard. In its December 5 edition, the *Boston Transcript* actually sided with the captain, stating:

> It is the general opinion among the residents and old mariners on Cape Cod that Capt. Blanchard never left port without orders, or at least against direct orders from the agent of the company. It is not the custom of captains of vessels to go against the orders of their superiors, especially in a case of this kind, and for that reason they believe that Capt. Blanchard, a dead man, had been unjustly condemned for the loss of his ship.

From the start, support for Blanchard had been almost almost universal within the seafaring community. Numerous New England ship captains expressed their feelings that, under the same circumstances, they would have acted exactly as he did. Captain Jason Collins was among the first to defend Blanchard's action. Collins, skipper of the steamer *Kennebec*, decided not to make the longer run from Boston to Gardiner, Maine, that evening and turned back shortly after sailing. He met *Portland* in Boston's lower harbor around seven-thirty Saturday evening. Collins said it should be remembered that *Portland* was a larger boat than *Kennebec* and was making a shorter run. Interestingly, when the matter of liability for the disaster was decided the following spring, the presiding district court judge, Nathan B. Webb, ruled that Liscomb did not order Blanchard to stay in port. Webb based his finding on Liscomb's own testimony, which avowed that the decision to sail "was left to the captain's discretion."

At 6:07 p.m., less than an hour before *Portland's* scheduled departure, the Weather Bureau office in Boston received word that it was still snowing in New York, but the wind had backed into the northwest.[1] To the weather-wise, it would be a sure sign the storm center had passed there

---

[1] This was a misleading, if not an incorrect report. A summary of local storm conditions issued from the Weather Bureau office in New York several weeks later stated that the wind did not shift to northwest until midnight. In fact, the storm's effects were felt long after this throughout the New York City area. Snow, which began Saturday afternoon, continued falling through the night, slackening off and ending prior to noontime on Sunday. Gale winds, ranging from 40 to 65 miles an hour, continued well into Sunday evening.

Thacher's Southern Light

and improving conditions were on the way. Momentarily, the Boston office telegraphed the report to the steamship line. If Blanchard were thinking at all seriously about going, the last-moment news would have been encouraging, especially since conditions in Boston were still good—no snow, sharp visibility, and only a light breeze.

At 7:00 p.m., *Portland* left India Wharf and sailed into eternity, taking 192 crew members and passengers with her.

The question of how far north *Portland* reached before either turning about or being forced off course by the storm has sparked considerable lively debate, particularly among those trying to conclude when the vessel sank. The late night Saturday sightings of the steamer off Cape Ann provide the last tangible clues, but they are conflicting and give only an approximate sense of the ship's track beyond its first two or three hours at sea.

The most northerly fix was made by Captain Lynes B. Hathaway, a master workman for the U.S. Lighthouse Service. Hathaway had been visiting the Thacher's Island light station and later told Boston newspapers that shortly after nine-thirty p.m., he watched *Portland's* lights as the steamship passed within 500 feet of Thacher's eastern shore. He said the vessel sailed between it and the Londoner, a dangerous, partially submerged reef less than 1,000 yards southeast of the island, and noted that nothing seemed unusual.

Thacher's is an approximately 80-acre island, one-half mile east of Cape Ann, belonging to the town of Rockport, Massachusetts. Because it lay directly along the commercial sailing route between Boston and ports in Maine,

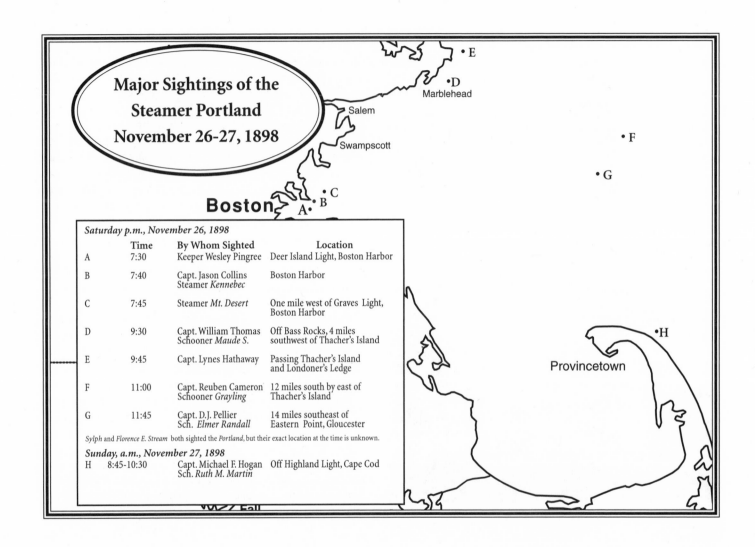

Major Sightings of the Steamer Portland November 26-27, 1898

E

D
Marblehead

Salem

Swampscott

F

G

C
Boston A• •B

H

Provincetown

	Saturday p.m., November 26, 1898		
	Time	**By Whom Sighted**	**Location**
A	7:30	Keeper Wesley Pingree	Deer Island Light, Boston Harbor
B	7:40	Capt. Jason Collins Steamer *Kennebec*	Boston Harbor
C	7:45	Steamer *Mt. Desert*	One mile west of Graves Light, Boston Harbor
D	9:30	Capt. William Thomas Schooner *Maude S.*	Off Bass Rocks, 4 miles southwest of Thacher's Island
E	9:45	Capt. Lynes Hathaway	Passing Thacher's Island and Londoner's Ledge
F	11:00	Capt. Reuben Cameron Schooner *Grayling*	12 miles south by east of Thacher's Island
G	11:45	Capt. D.J. Pellier Sch. *Elmer Randall*	14 miles southeast of Eastern Point, Gloucester

Sylph and *Florence E. Stream* both sighted the *Portland*, but their exact location at the time is unknown.

	Sunday, a.m., November 27, 1898		
H	8:45-10:30	Capt. Michael F. Hogan Sch. *Ruth M. Martin*	Off Highland Light, Cape Cod

FOUR SHORT BLASTS

Canada, and Europe, local residents soon decided it was a critical spot for a prominent navigational aid. Their request to the General Court of Massachusetts resulted in the construction of twin, stone lighthouses, each 45-feet high, on the northeast side of the island. The two beacons went into operation in December 1771, making Thacher's the eleventh and last light station constructed during British rule of the American colonies.

That *Portland* passed Thacher's with no apparent trouble indicates the ship had routinely covered nearly one-third of the overnight trip to Maine. How much farther north it traveled is only guesswork. There is evidence the steamer was seen again in the next two hours, although exactly where and when is subject to debate. The captains of at least three schooners scrambling to make Gloucester harbor told Boston newspaper reporters they encountered *Portland* between eleven p.m. and midnight—by their estimates, some 2 1/2 to 14 miles southeast of Cape Ann. Confronting rapidly rising winds and intensifying snow, the smaller fishing vessels were struggling through mounting seas and poor visibility, out of sight of land and navigational aids. The reports of their precise locations at the times of the sightings is thus doubtful. Under such conditions, how accurately could the sailors have reckoned their bearings, and how likely were any to have checked their pocket watches at the moment *Portland* hove into view?

When *Portland* failed to arrive at Franklin Wharf as scheduled Sunday morning, speculation rather than concern about its whereabouts was the rule, and it varied greatly. At first, the general consensus was the vessel had sought shelter in such harbors as Gloucester, Portsmouth, or Provincetown. But when contact with these communities proved this was not the case, there were many who suggested a variety of far-flung possibilities.

Captain Colby, skippering the steamship *State of Maine* during its Sunday trip from Maine to Boston, kept a sharp watch for *Portland* en route, but saw no trace of the ship. Colby told the *Boston Globe,* "I think that Capt. Blanchard may have been forced to run to the eastward as far as Isle au Haut, and that he may be slowly steaming back." Colby's veteran pilot, Captain Garnett, disagreed, saying he believed "that if any trace is to be found of the steamship, it would be found on the Georges (an offshore fishing bank extending more than 150 miles northeastward from the outer end of Nantucket Shoals). Some fishermen there might have seen her driving in the storm. A steamer looking for her should go well out."

These kinds of statements ended abruptly when wreckage from *Portland* began piling up on Cape Cod late Monday night. At that point, the overlying question became: When and where did the steamer go down?

The intriguing uncertainty about the location of *Portland's* foundering and the time it occurred has, over time, resulted in three schools of thought. The first, as reported in contemporary newspapers, contended that the ship sank Sunday morning, anywhere from one to ten miles off the northern tip of Cape Cod. Later, the writings of Thomas Harrison Eames and Edward Rowe Snow suggested a Sunday night sinking within a narrower band—five to eight miles from the same stretch of shore. In the

Portland in the height of the gale. No lifeboats ever washed ashore and is it highly unlikely that an attempt was made to launch one in the force of the gale as this painting depicts.

FOUR SHORT BLASTS

1980s, the Historical Maritime Group of New England conducted a rigorous scientific investigation, augmented by sophisticated electronic technology, of the ocean floor across a wide portion of Massachusetts Bay. In 1989, it offered a body of new evidence that places the steamer's final resting place some 20 miles north of the Cape, which might also indicate a morning sinking is more credible.

The alternate notions whether *Portland* went down in the morning or the evening have evolved because watches found on the bodies of several victims were stopped between nine and ten o'clock. The one taken from Mrs. Jennie G. Edmonds, who was discovered at Orleans, read 9:17. Since *Portland* had ostensibly been seen after ten o'clock Saturday night and its wreckage began piling up onshore before midnight Sunday, it left only two logical possibilities—Sunday a.m. or p.m.

Portland's double-clappered engine room gong

The likelihood that *Portland* was still afloat past Sunday morning was bolstered by Captain Michael Francis Hogan of the fishing schooner *Ruth M. Martin*. Hogan, trying to nurse the disabled schooner into Provincetown, claimed that between eight and nine o'clock that morning, he spotted a sidewheel steamer off Highland Light. He stated that he could see the ship—under power, with its head to the seas—for about two hours, until the two vessels finally drifted far enough apart that the failing visibility obstructed further view. If Hogan's observation is valid, *Portland* was still afloat after ten a.m. and would thus have gone down that night.

From the first, the Boston papers declared that *Portland* had foundered in the morning, and Captain Hogan's sighting—which was known but not widely reported of until December 6—did nothing to alter the contention.

One of the newspaper arguments in favor of the Sunday morning sinking theory presumed that *Portland* would have run out of fuel by then and, unable to make further headway, would have breached to. In this vulnerable state, the heavy seas would have made short work of the ship, crashing across the decks, tearing away at the superstructure, eventually flooding the interior and sending the lurching hull on its final, sickening downward plunge.

In fact, when *Portland* left India Wharf Saturday evening, it carried approximately 65 tons of coal. It was steamship company policy to fuel the vessel each time it arrived in Portland, and mate Edward Deering had supervised the process prior to the Friday departure. Leaving Franklin Wharf on November 25, *Portland* had aboard 90 tons of coal—83 in the bunkers, with seven more heaped on deck.

The steamer customarily burned about 25 tons of fuel during the nine-hour run between Boston and Portland—slightly less than three tons per hour. At that rate, the remaining 65 would theoretically have lasted another 23 hours, or roughly until six o'clock Sunday evening. Beyond that, as Thomas Harrison Eames surmised, the vessel might have continued under steam even longer, if the crew had broken up the furnishings and interior fixtures—maybe even the freight—to feed the fires.

During the early 1940s, authors Eames and Snow, in separate stories, suggested the idea of a Sunday night, closer-to-shore sinking. Both cited Captain Hogan's alleged visual encounter with *Portland* as evidence for the later moment, and Snow added the argument that such great masses of the steamer's wreckage would not have piled onshore as they did—within a half-mile stretch, in a matter of a few hours—had the vessel sunk more than a few miles offshore.

A section of oar which washed ashore when *Portland* foundered.

The inshore/offshore debate has primarily been predicated on where remains of the steamer have been found. Initial public opinion centered on Peaked Hill Bar, off Race Point, since it was directly opposite these treacherous shoal waters where the first and greatest concentration of debris washed in. In the hours and days following the tragedy, additional remains were tossed up along Cape beaches farther south, but these were thought to have been carried there by the prevailing ocean currents.

Early in his investigation of the *Portland* sinking, Snow concluded that the ship lay not too far from Cape Cod. In his 1943 book *Great Storms and Famous Shipwrecks of the New England Coast*, he wrote: "If such a heaping pile of wreckage (found by the life-savers near Race Point) travelled even ten miles (before reaching the beach), it would have been scattered up and down the shore." Snow also contended that the movement of flotsam would have been controlled by the prevailing wind and surface waves. He pointed out that the wind direction at each of the life-saving stations from Race Point to Pamet River, overnight Sunday into Monday, was reported as northerly, with high waves coming in from the northeast. Under these conditions, he maintained, objects cast into the sea from a point more than seven or eight miles off the northern tip of the Cape would carry past Race Point and come ashore along the southwestern shores of Cape Cod Bay. According to him, no such finds were reported.

Over the years, Snow came to believe that *Portland* sank some 5 1/2 miles north of Highland Light, in water less than 150 feet deep. His conviction stemmed from Captain Charles Carver's 1924 discovery of what the captain and others believed was irrefutable evidence of the steamer's principal remains. Snow ultimately financed and organized a diving expedition in June of 1945, which he claimed located the steamer's hull, resting on its beam ends, 144 feet down.

In April 1949, Commander Henry C. Nichols, USNR, a repair officer at the Boston Naval Shipyard, bolstered the Snow theory. Nichols believed that during the Sunday morning lull in the storm, the crew aboard *Portland* sighted the Highlands, at Cape Cod, and using the prominent landmark as a fix, set a course for Boston. On this heading the ship would have passed across the southwest corner of Stellwagen Bank—the very spot where Snow's diver Al George said he located the wreck five years before. Nichols declared that *Portland* "got into the breakers" in the relatively shallow water here, "and that was her end."

Commander Nichols related that following World War I, he was stationed aboard a temporary lightship on Stellwagen Bank. A veteran boatswain and former fisherman serving with him had seen this shoal area "breaking white" on several occasions, even though it is normally covered by as much as 50 feet of water. Nichols believed the November 1898 storm would have created these same conditions.

On the other hand, others have since studied the storm and its mechanics at length and are convinced that *Portland* went down in deeper water, much farther north. In 1989, the Historical Maritime Group of New England, which had been actively searching for *Portland's* remains for more than a decade, publicly announced it had at last located them in more than 300 feet of water. Using an underwater camera, HMG members made several photographs of the wreck site, some 20 miles north of Cape Cod, and described some of the images they made as showing portions of the ship's stern section.[2]

The question: "How many victims did *Portland's* sinking claim?" has been another enigma, complicated principally by the fact there was no copy of the vessel's passenger list ashore. The only existing roster was in the possession of the ship's purser, Frederick A. Ingraham, and it was never recovered among the ship"s wreckage which washed ashore. After more than 30 years of gathering stories from people claiming to have lost relatives or friends aboard the steamer, Edward Rowe Snow dryly commented that if they were all true, the ship surely would have sunk at India Wharf before sailing from the sheer weight of the more than 8,000 additional passengers.

Initial newspaper reports of casualties, based on the Portland Steamship Company's first estimate, ran to fewer than 100. Within 72 hours, however, so many concerned family members and friends of those supposedly aboard had bombarded the firm's offices in Boston and Portland for news of their loved ones' fate, it became obvious there were far more. The *Boston Globe* printed a roster in its December 2 editions that showed 107 passengers and 63 crew members—170 souls in all. Subsequent revisions during the next week increased the total to 176—one additional passenger and five more crew. That figure was routinely accepted until 1956, when Edward Rowe Snow issued a widely-circulated plea to anyone who might have information about others still not among the "official" tally. As a result, another 14 names were added, and in the early 1960s, a fifteenth, bringing the most reliable count to 191.[3]

The name of Captain Burke Dunbar of Penobscot, Maine, was added after his descendants contacted Snow to report that Dunbar had clambered aboard the steamer after the gangplank had been hauled aboard, throwing his suitcase up over the rail and "making a jump for it" just as the ship was easing

---

[2] Snow's claim to locating the hulk of the *Portland* and the findings of the Historical Maritime Group of New England are discussed in further detail in Chapter Seven of this volume.

[3] Research for this book raised the definitive count to 192 persons after a complete reexamination of newspapers of the time and a study of subsequent claims by family members and of letters received by the authors from descendants of those aboard the *Portland*.

Alphonse Gosselin
Montreal, Canada

Ruth Frye
Portland. Maine

Isaiah Frye
Portland, Maine

William H. Roche
Portland, Maine

Mrs. Horace Pratt
Portland, Maine

Frank F. Richardson
Cambridge, Massachusetts

Emily L. Cobb
Portland, Maine

Dudley E. Freeman
Yarmouth, Maine

A selection of newspaper portraits of Portland *passengers*

Four Short Blasts

away from the wharf. The reason for his haste was the birth of a new son, Karl Burke Dunbar, and the young father was more than a little eager to return home to be with him. Captain Dunbar's remains were eventually discovered on Cape Cod and shipped back to Penobscot for burial.

Another question that has been raised is whether *Portland* may have gone down after colliding with another vessel. At least three ships have been mentioned as possibilities in such involvement, although there's no real evidence with any to support the speculation.

On December 1, 1898, the *Boston Globe* published a lengthy statement from someone it labeled "a well-known sea captain," who said: "in my belief, the (schooner) *King Philip*...and the *Portland*...came together in the thick darkness (Sunday night) without a moment's warning and both went to the bottom." In hindsight, this seems a rather remote possibility, since the first pieces of *King Philip's* wreckage did not come ashore until long after *Portland's* debris washed in. A steam pump identified as belonging to the big four-master landed on the beach at Brewster, on the inside of the Cape, two or three days after *Portland's* remains were discovered. Then, on December 12, a portion of the schooner's badly broken stern section, showing the letters "—hilip, Balt., Md.," came up on Great Island, near Wellfleet.

Edward Rowe Snow felt inclined to believe the possibility that *Portland* may have been struck by the granite-laden schooner *Addie E. Snow*. Snow cited the fact the 162-ton vessel's medicine chest and other articles were discovered among the mounds of debris from *Portland*. He also claimed that diver Al George, exploring in 1945 what Snow thought was *Portland's* wreck site, located what he said were *Addie E. Snow's* remains nearby. Despite the claim, no conclusive proof of George's alleged discovery is known to exist.

Occasional fragments of the steamer *Pentagoet* were also located within the greatest concentration of *Portland's* wreckage. Most significant was the upper part of *Pentagoet's* cabin, painted the distinctive deep red hue that distinguished the vessel's entire superstructure. This discovery, coupled with Captain Hogan's professed sighting of both vessels off Highland Light Sunday morning, November 27, has fueled some speculation that the two steamers may ultimately have collided in the storm. However, none of the bodies of *Pentagoet's* 18 passengers and crew were ever found, and it seems likely that had the two vessels struck, bodies from both would have come ashore, instead of just from *Portland*.

Some of those reported as lost when *Portland* went down, later turned up safe. A Miss Burns was delayed getting to the wharf Saturday evening and instead took Monday's 9:00 a.m. train. A number of others had intended to sail, but decided not to go because of the threatening weather. Mr. & Mrs. Albert Trickey later returned home to Westbrook by train; Mrs. H.W. Dukeshire, Captain J.E. Lindsay, and Malcolm W. Lindsay, all of Portland, waited until the following week to travel back to Maine by rail.

Several members of *Portland's* crew avoided the tragedy for various reasons. George Watson, the second cook, had gone to St. John, New Brunswick, to attend his mother's funeral and didn't get back to Portland in time to make the November 25 departure. Saloonmen Charles H. Johnson and William Dunn had quit their jobs only two weeks before the disaster. First pilot Louis F. Strout, first mate Edward B. Deering, and purser's clerk J.F. Hunt made the Friday trip to Boston, but remained in town to attend the funeral of Captain Charles Deering. Steward Lewis W.A. Johnson simply missed the boat when it left Portland on Friday. Family tradition maintains he over-imbibed prior to sailing, and by the time he reached the wharf, the steamer had already left the dock and was gliding down the harbor.

A few passengers sailed without being able to tell friends or relatives they would be aboard, and their fate was unknown for days afterward. Jes Jessen Schmidt[4], his wife Jessine, and their two sons, Jorgen and Anton, had just returned from a visit to Denmark, the family's homeland. They arrived in Boston on the steamer *Dominion* only hours before *Portland* sailed. After passing through customs, the four decided to continue on to Maine that evening via boat. Hans Jessen Schmidt, Jessen's brother in Portland, had been anticipating the family's return for some time and grew increasingly concerned after learning of the tragedy. In early December, he contacted the U.S. Immigration Commissioner's office in Boston, where he was informed of the Schmidts' plans to sail aboard *Portland* the night of the 26th.

In the days following the disaster, numerous accounts surfaced about those who decided at the last minute not to go.[5] One who did change her mind was Mrs. Anna M Young, of Boston, who told a *Herald* reporter:

I was resting in my stateroom. The whistle of the Portland was sounding for all visitors to go ashore. Suddenly there was a knock at the door, and a message from my mother was delivered. Mother believed a storm was coming, and she had a premonition that I shouldn't sail. Carrying my child, I ran for the gangplank just as they started to lift it, and they waited for me. When I got ashore I heard the final whistle of the *Portland* as she left the wharf.

The story of the ship's cat deciding not to sail has been retold many times, with various embellishments. Today, it is hard to know how much of it, if any, is true. One version relates that a Maine man, waiting to board the steamer, noticed the feline busily carrying her kittens off the ship to a nearby shed. Back and forth she went, between boat and dock, until she had deposited the entire litter ashore. The man decided what he had seen was an ill omen and decided to stay the night in Boston.

During the great November gale, tremendous seas made

---

[4] Jessen, Jes Jessen Schmidt's middle name, goes back to 1760 in this Danish family's history. Reuel Jessen Smith of Santa Rosa, California, Jes Jessen Schmidt's grand nephew and the eighth Jessen in the family, was named Jessen to memorialize for another generation the Schmidt family's loss aboard *Portland*.

[5] In June of 1998, as this book was going to press, the authors received a letter from a Cape Elizabeth, Maine resident saying that her grandmother, Annie Cotton Burdenkin and her grandmother's son, Reginald Burdenkin, had boarded the *Portland* in Boston and then, at the urging of relatives, had their luggage put back on the pier and had disembarked.

Above, Hans Jessen Schmidt of Deering, Maine, and his family. Right, a letter from the Immigration Commissioner in Boston notifying Hans Jessen Schmidt that his brother Jes Jessen Schmidt and his family probably went down with the *Portland*. A bronze tablet in South Portland's Forest City Cemetery marks the Schmidt family's loss.

No. 3008.   Office of U. S. Commissioner of Immigration,

No. 70 Long Wharf, Boston,

Dec. 3, 1898.

Hans Schmidt, Esq.,

Deering, Maine.

Dear Sir:-

On S/S "Dominion" that arrived at this port Nov. 26th, were the following named family,

Jessen Schmidt, aged 32,
Jessine   "   "   28,
Jorgen   "   "   5,
Anton   "   "   4.

Mr. Schmidt informed us that he was going to his brother in Deering, Maine, by the Portland boat that was to leave that evening. As the S/S "Portland" was wrecked that evening, I write to inquire if the Schmidt family reached you, for if they did not the probability is that they went down with the S/S "Portland".

Kindly let me hear from you at your earliest convenience.

Respectfully yours,

Geo. B. Billings
Commissioner.

IN MEMORY OF
JES. J. SMITH
AGE 32
HIS WIFE AND TWO SONS
LOST ON S/S PORTLAND
BOSTON TO PORTLAND
NOV. 26 - 1898.

unusual inroads into the dunes above many sections of Cape Cod beach, scouring out hundreds of thousands of yards of sand and greatly altering the contour of the shorefront. Many of those who searched for bodies believed that dozens more *Portland* victims were hidden deep beneath the sands soon after they washed up, as were doors and other parts of the ill-fated steamer which were later dug up from three feet or more below the surface.

The bodies of only 40 passengers and crew were ever found, 36 of whom were discovered on Cape Cod within two weeks of the disaster. Many had been entombed in the sand soon after they came ashore, only to be uncovered by wave action in succeeding days. A powerful northeast storm on December 4 disinterred the remains of several, including those of Lewis J. Metcalf. On December 6, surfman Burch, from the Race Point Life-Saving Station, unexpectedly came upon Metcalf's sanded-in body. Burch reported it was nowhere to be seen during his westbound patrol, but was partially uncovered by the time he made the return trip.

As the grim search for victims continued, state legislators and other government officials in Boston grew increasingly critical of Portland Steamship officials for not joining the ongoing efforts, either to locate bodies or hunt for wreckage. On December 10, the *Boston Globe* reported, "There is a strong feeling against the steamship company at the state house. The tone of indignation is unmistakable." Dr. Joshua F. Lewis of the Board of Charity accused the company of doing practically nothing. In separate remarks to the *Globe*, Lewis scolded, "...the company says it

will send divers when the ship is found. Why should not the company find the ship?"

Concerned that bodies might still be floating at sea, but steadily drifting further from where they would ever be discovered, Dr. Lewis appealed directly to Massachusetts Governor Roger Wolcott for immediate help in initiating a water search. Lewis asked the governor to authorize the use of a small steamer to cruise the waters south and east of Cape Cod, where objects from *Portland* might have carried.

Governor Wolcott granted the request, and the following Monday the tug *Herald*, in command of Captain A.L. Hersey, left Boston with a search team consisting of police captain W.H. Proctor and detectives F.A. Rhoades and L.G. Burleigh. Two newspaper reporters accompanied the official party. Poor visibility kept the group at Provincetown overnight Monday. Early Tuesday, Captain Hersey maneuvered the tug—with the three officers intently scanning the waters either side of the ship—past Highland Light, Nauset, Orleans, and Chatham, then on to the Pollock Rip, Handkerchief, and Shoveful lightships, before putting in at Hyannis for the night.

On Wednesday, Hersey followed the shoals south to Nantucket, before working east to the Great Round Shoal lightship, then north to Monomoy and west, back to Hyannis. Thursday morning, he steamed toward Vineyard Sound, then seesawed back around the elbow and arm of the Cape, eventually arriving in Boston at 10:15 that night. Although *Herald* had covered 392 miles, the search team failed to find a single body or see "so much as a splinter from the wreck."

The *Herald* search essentially convinced those hoping to retrieve additional victims that further offshore exploration would be futile. It seemed increasingly unlikely the sea would give up any more of *Portland's* dead, nor would it willingly yield the secrets of the steamer's fatal trip.

The question which no one can answer, then or now, is: "What was happening aboard *Portland* as the steamer was tossed to and fro in the gale?"

A clue as to conditions at sea during the storm is found in the recollections of George and Martha Weeks, who were returning to Maine aboard *Portland* from a honeymoon trip to Boston two weeks prior to the great Thanksgiving weekend gale. In later years they told their recollections of the voyage to their grandson, historian William B. Jordan, Jr.

According to Jordan, his grandmother was so frightened by the pitching, rolling and groaning of the ship that she never changed into her night clothes and refused to go to bed. Equally disturbing was the clearly audible ringing of the engine room gong, which was sounding to signal the engine room crew to change the vessel's speed. Her new husband, who had been a ticket taker as a boy on the Boston steamers, could interpret the gong signals and was quite concerned, but did not share this anxiety with his wife until their trip was over and they were safely ashore in Portland.

What the Weeks endured was probably only a strong coastal blow; it certainly was not a major gale. The storm experienced by the *Portland's* passengers and crew could only have been a rolling, surging, thrusting nightmare. Hurtling to the left, lifting her exposed right paddlewheel out of the water, the steamer would rotate back to the right, creating a giant vibration as the descending paddlewheel thundered and blasted its way lower and lower into the unforgiving sea. On and on it went … the roaring wind creating sounds like thunderclaps which reverberated in the pounding ears of the men, women and children being thrown about below.

To the officers in the pilothouse the giant waves accelerating toward *Portland* could only have appeared as mountains hurling themselves across a dark seascape—mountains moving to crush or tear apart the vessel's superstructure and then drive her hulk to the bottom of the Atlantic.

Below, chairs, chamber pots, dishes, luggage and hundreds of other ordinary objects would have shot uncontrolled, projectile-like, across staterooms, down dark passageways, and athwart the steamer's public areas, dealing nipping blows to anyone displaced by the surging sea into their trajectories.

Eventually the humanity aboard would have attempted to save themselves and their loved ones by struggling into cork-filled life preservers, all the while being scourged by the thundering noise; and flung indiscriminately at the bulkhead, the floor, the ceiling—or at all of those three-dimensional obstructions.

Before long, men, women and children were either swept overboard to perish in the sea, or even more horrific, trapped below decks, enshrined in some angle of the expiring craft.

The foundering of *Portland*.

FOUR SHORT BLASTS

THE AFTERMATH
Legal Hearing Into The Loss of *Portland*

Following the *Portland* sinking, Massachusetts Representative John Fitzgerald introduced a resolution in the U.S. House instructing the Secretary of the Treasury to investigate the circumstances surrounding the loss of the steamship. Fitzgerald's December 5 bill directed the agency:

> ...to determine whether due care and vigilance were exercised by the officials of the company owning and controlling that steamer in allowing her to proceed to sea on the evening of November 26, and to make particular inquiry in regard to the condition of the lifeboats and life preservers used upon this steamer.

Despite the initiative, no formal government inquest into the disaster ever took place. Because there were no survivors, the U.S. Steam-Boat Inspection Service, which normally oversaw such matters, had no obligation to get involved, and thus did not. If any blame for the tragedy were to be assessed and restitution made, it would have to result from civil litigation originating with relatives and friends of the victims against the steamship company. This action was not long in coming.

On December 23, 1898, a suit was filed against the Portland Steamship Company. It was brought by Portland attorney Samuel L. Bates for Nathan Cohen, father of Samuel Cohen, one of the passengers aboard the steamer and administrator of his estate. The writ charged general negligence on the part of the steamship company, alleging that *Portland* was not properly equipped for winter service and claiming the line showed recklessness for permitting the steamer to leave Boston on such a night. Other indictments referred to the inadequate condition of the vessel and the state of the life preservers, lifeboats, and other gear. Almost simultaneously, a similar suit was brought by William H. Looney, attorney for Mr. Edward L. Baker, on behalf of Baker's wife, Beulah, another victim of the sinking.

For its part, the Portland Steamship Company formally denied all liability for the disaster and on December 26 asked the U.S. District Court in Portland to decree that none existed. Benjamin Thompson, one of the firm's attorneys, filed a petition to limit the company's obligation for the loss of the steamship and to block all further filings against it. District court judge Nathan B. Webb declined the plea, saying he did not propose to shut the door to any other legitimate parties who wished to claim damages at a future time.

The next day, the court appointed William Leavitt as trustee of the steamship. In doing so, it instructed the company to transfer "its interest in said steamer *Portland*, her boilers, engines, tackle, apparel, and furniture, together with the freight pending at the time of said loss" to Mr. Leavitt. Judge Webb then instructed Leavitt to seek any and all information that would lead him to locate the wrecked vessel and secure all property belonging to it. Leavitt was to report his findings to the court no later than April 15, 1899.

Webb also directed that a monition, or warning, be issued against all persons claiming damages growing out of the loss of the steamship, citing them to appear before his court and "make due proof of their respective claims on or before the 30th day of March 1899, at twelve o'clock noon...or be forever barred from so doing." When the cut-off date arrived, district court commissioner William M. Bradley had received 55 claims against the steamship line, amounting to a total of $494,626.00. The compensation sought by the individual litigants ranged from $5,000 to $10,500. In each instance, $5,000 was asked for the loss of life; in 44 of these, an additional $5,000 was sought for bodily and mental pain; and in 41, from $35 to $500, for the loss of personal property.

At Judge Webb's further direction, commissioner Bradley ordered each claimant to file answers to the steamship company's petition—as well as costs for bonds—by 2:00 p.m., May 1. He then suspended further action on all claims until mid-May, when the Portland Steamship Company would have its own day in court, to offer supporting evidence of its limited liability petition.

In the meantime, William Leavitt filed his trustee's report on April 1, in which he stated in part:

> Since my said appointment I have kept constantly on the lookout for any information which may lead to the location of the steamer *Portland*, with a view of examining the surroundings determining whether any action on my part would result in preserving any part thereof for the interests of the parties concerned in said cause, but up to this time there has not been any information received by me of a character which in my judgment would warrant my making any effort to find or locate said vessel.
>
> From the reports which I have received, I am satisfied that said steamer foundered in such deep water that it will be impossible to adopt any measures which can successfully result in saving anything of value to the parties who may eventually be entitled thereto.

On May 16, the court proceedings resumed. One by one, the various petitioners, or their attorneys, appeared and announced they wished to drop their suits against the steamship line, indicating a willingness to "concede the legal impregnability of the company's position." The court consented, and the challenges against the steamship company evaporated.

Even as the charges were being dismissed, Portland Steamship Company attorney Thompson was before the court, reading the firm's petition for a limitation of its liability and calling a long succession of witnesses to uphold the claim there was, in fact, no obligation at all. Those testifying included several officials from The New England Company, which had built the steamer; agent George F. Morse of the Portland Company, which had installed the ship's machinery; general manager John F. Liscomb, agent Charles F. Williams, and others from the Portland Steamship Company, owners of the vessel.

Second pilot Lewis Nelson and first mate Edward B. Deering, officers of *Portland* who escaped the disaster because Captain Blanchard had given them permission to attend the funeral of former *Bay State* skipper Charles Deering, were also called. So were Captains Merritt and Pollister, inspectors from the U.S. Steam-Boat Inspection Service; Captains William W. Cook and Samuel O. Fisher of the U.S. Life-Saving Service stations at Race Point and Peaked Hill Bars, respectively, as well as members of their crews; Captains A.M. Miles and George W. Bunker, master mariners caught at sea off the New England coast during the November 26-27 storm; U.S. Lighthouse Service personnel Lynes B. Hathaway and William Harrington, visiting at Thacher's Island the night of the blow; and Boon Island lighthouse keeper William C. Williams.

Those involved with the ship's construction spoke highly of it. New England Company superintendent Amos B. Haggett suggested "the work was done as good as it could be done" and could not see how it could have been any better. William Melcher, who already had 36 years of experience as a master joiner with the firm when *Portland* was built, said he felt the ship's specifications were quite exacting and "think we lived up to them." Portland Company agent George Morse declared his firm had previously built six or eight engines like the one it fashioned for *Portland* and never had any doubt the work was "well done," noting he had never had a complaint about it during the nearly nine years it operated.

George Johnson, an engineer with the steamship com-

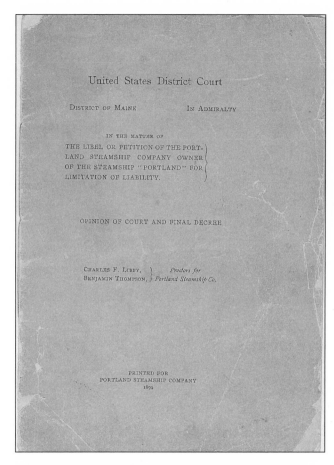

A rare copy of *The Opinion of the Court and Final Decree* in the case of the loss of the steamer *Portland*.

pany since 1853, testified he had been aboard *Portland* as chief engineer from August 1889 until February 1894. He believed the ship's boilers and engine were of "first quality." Speaking of the steamer's seaworthiness, he stated it "was a good sea-going vessel and could make headway against the wind when other vessels failed."

General manager Liscomb testified that for several years he had been in charge of repairs to the company's ships, "upon which no limitations of expense had ever been placed." He affirmed that *Portland* was hauled for six to eight weeks each spring, while necessary maintenance and repairs were made prior to the annual federal inspection. During these times the vessel was in charge of William Davis, who had overseen the original construction on behalf of the company. At the request of the court, Davis went into great technical detail explaining how *Portland's* hull and decks had been built. He stated that he watched the timber put into the ship—three-inch, white oak planking above the water line and four-inch, southern pine below. He concluded his remarks by saying that in the spring of 1898, he went over the ship thoroughly, fore and aft, testing it with a hammer and making numerous borings throughout, concluding it was "in an excellent and seaworthy condition."

Captain Pollister of the Steam-Boat Inspection Service then affirmed that he had inspected *Portland* in May 1898, and "found the steamer all right." He spoke about how the ship was undergoing minor repairs when he examined it and felt that as a result, "the boat was made even better...and the hull even stronger than when she was new." A local

newspaper reporter found Pollister's remarks "very important and interesting, showing as it did that the *Portland*...was in absolutely perfect and seaworthy condition."

General manager Liscomb was called back to speak about the steamer's life-saving gear, which he swore was ample, in full compliance with regulations, and "in perfect order." He asserted that *Portland* carried eight metal lifeboats, four metal life rafts, and 758 cork-filled life jackets. Company attorney Benjamin Thompson confirmed Liscomb's statement, adding that when new, the white steamer had been equipped with 660 jackets, and later received 115 more.[1]

Liscomb and Thompson's testimony contradicted and ultimately laid to rest earlier conjecture, particularly in Boston newspapers, that *Portland* may have been carrying inadequate "tule" life preservers. These were a type filled

---

[1]The Pilgrim Monument and Provincetown Museum owns the life preserver, shown above, which washed ashore after the Portland's foundering. It clearly displays it's original "Str. *Portland*" black stenciling, leaving no question as to its authenticity. Researching this book, the authors were allowed to closely examine this life preserver by Jeffory Morris, Museum Curator. A hole in the preserver's fabric allowed us to see the contents— small pieces of granulated cork.

Tremont took over *Portland's* duties on the Portland to Boston run after it was apparent that *Portland* had foundered.

The sparkling *Governor Dingley,* a steel screw propeller vessel, replaced *Tremont* on the Portland to Boston run in 1899.

FOUR SHORT BLASTS

with tule grass—a reed from one- to three-quarters of an inch in diameter which grows on the Pacific coast—and bound with copper wire. Scoffed at in the papers as containing little more than "dried grass," tule preservers had been proven incapable of sustaining the same weight as those of cork and lost their buoyant characteristic once the tule had become water-soaked for any length of time. As Liscomb and Thompson pointed out, however, tule-filled life preservers were manufactured only in belt form, while the more substantial jacket style—as *Portland* carried—contained the preferable cork filling.

At the conclusion of the steamship company's two days of evidence, Judge Webb issued a lengthy opinion and final decree, in which he declared the loss of *Portland* "an act of God and beyond their (the steamship company's) ability to guard against." Webb ordered the Portland Steamship Company to pay $10.00 to trustee William Leavitt and $50.00 to commissioner William Bradley, for their services, and to absorb the various fees, costs, and charges due the court's clerk and marshal. Beyond that, he declared the case closed.

Portland's tragic loss marked the end of side-wheel steamship construction for coastal passage. The following year, Portland Steamship Company management replaced the ship with the steel screw propeller *Governor Dingley* and, in 1900, sold *Tremont* to the New York-based Joy Line. After the firm was absorbed into the Eastern Steamship Company consolidation of 1901, the latter rebuilt *Bay State*, widening the beam, replacing the radial paddle wheels with newer feathering ones, and lowering the paddle shaft.

Eastern's sister ships *Camden* (1907) and *Belfast* (1909) represented further advancement in steamship construction and technology. These were triple screw, turbine-type vessels, with 320-foot steel hulls having almost no overhang in the guards, and amply suited for whatever conditions they would face during a subsequent quarter century of use in New England waters.

The Portland Steamship Company learned another painful lesson. Henceforth, duplicate copies of the crew and passenger lists for all trips by each of its vessels would routinely be kept on shore—a practice adopted by other lines, as well. Fortunately, it was a precaution that would rarely have to be called into play. Aside from minor mishaps which claimed an occasional vessel and prompted the rescue of stranded passengers and crews, twentieth century steamship travel in New England waters never witnessed anything approaching the terrible tragedy that befell the steamer *Portland* in November 1898.

Detail of a model of the *Portland* made by George Elliott of Waterford, Maine, which clearly shows the vessel's exposed paddle guards and the vulnerability of the wheel itself to the forces of a tremendous gale.

The Legend Continues
Edward Rowe Snow Keeps The *Portland* Saga Alive

News of the *Portland* sinking continued to dominate front-page headlines in New England newspapers for more than a week after the disaster. As each passing day brought word that more victims' bodies had washed up along the outer Cape Cod beaches, interest continued to heighten as to where and how the vessel had met its fate. That speculation has continued in the minds of many people ever since and has resulted in a series of attempts to locate the steamship's hull and settle the mystery for good.

The *Boston Globe* made the first determined attempt to learn the truth when it financed a week-long undertaking in early December and placed Navy Lieutenant Nicholas J. Halpine in charge. Halpine was commander of the U.S. Hydrographic Office in Boston and considered as knowledgeable as any to conduct the quest. The *Globe* wanted Halpine to explore the ocean bottom in the area known as Peaked Hill Bar, a nearly mile-long finger of submerged sand about five miles northeast of Race Point. Roughly 1,000 yards offshore, the underwater dunes were covered by an average of only 16 to 18 feet of water at low tide. It was opposite these dangerous shallows that the initial fragments of *Portland* wreckage came ashore, and *Globe* man-

Lt. Nicholas J. Halpine, USN

agement wanted to prove conclusively whether the steamer did or did not founder here.

Lieutenant Halpine chartered the Boston harbor tugs *A.W. Chesterton* and *W.H. Gallison* and equipped them with crews, divers, and the necessary search apparatus. The expedition sailed from Boston harbor in the wee hours of Thursday, December 8. Arriving off Provincetown before daybreak, the tiny convoy found the seas along the outer Cape far too treacherous to begin work. In fact, contrary conditions would prevent any exploration until the following Monday.

In the interim, Halpine hired the 45-foot, Provincetown fishing schooner *Ella Nash* to assist in the hunt. Halpine had devised a scheme whereby the two tugs would sail in tandem—about a quarter mile apart—dragging a length of heavy chain between them. *Ella Nash* would remain astern the pair, with its cable and anchor attached to the center of the chain. This would give the drag additional weight and keep it on the bottom. Halpine envisioned that if the chain snagged anything, the schooner would anchor, marking the spot, while the tugs rounded in and hauled up the lines. The schooner would then send down a diver, to identify the "catch."

Chapter Seven

Monday's weather proved little better than it had been over the weekend. The seas continued to run high, and light snow made the visibility fuzzy, adding to the uncertainty of maintaining good bearings. But with the forecast of a major storm for the following day, Lieutenant Halpine was determined to get started without further delay. The search team was up well before daylight and in position off Race Point by nine a.m.

According to Halpine's plan, each of the tugs payed out 300 fathoms (1,800 feet) of hawser, attached to its end of the drag chain. *Ella Nash's* 30-fathom (180-foot) chain had been bent at the center to one of its anchors—with the stock removed—and attached to the drag. The anchor would thus be towed with the crown forward, pulling the schooner with it. Beginning at the Peaked Hill Bar whistling buoy and working east, *Gallison*—having the shallower draft—maintained a course closer to the shore, while *Chesterton* steamed along to seaward. The procession traveled at a very slow speed, enabling the entire drag and the majority of the tow cable to stay on the bottom. The maneuver effectively spanned more than 1,200 feet at a single pass.

During the sweep the two tugs used a special signal code to communicate. From the Peaked Hill Bars Life-Saving Station, lookouts at one point heard the vessels whistling back and forth and thought they might need assistance. Captain William W. Cook and the life-savers launched a surfboat and went to investigate, only to discover the false alarm.

By three p.m. light snow, which had fallen intermittently through the day, grew steadily heavier and caused Lieu-

The December 15, 1898 *Boston Globe* featured the *Globe* financed search for *Portland's* hull on the Peaked Hill Bar.

tenant Halpine to halt the operation. The six-hour search had encompassed an area from the Race Point Life-Saving Station to High Head and from near shore to a depth of eight fathoms. Outside Peaked Hill Bar, the tugs carefully zigzagged seaward to 13 fathoms. The hunt failed to turn up even the slightest hint of any wreckage.

Tuesday's weather was too poor to permit work, and the forecast called for little or no improvement in the foreseeable future. The search vessels sailed out from Provincetown early in the morning, but returned after getting only as far as Race Point. At that, the *Globe* officials aboard conferred with Lieutenant Halpine and decided to abandon the expedition. In an article in its December 15 editions, the paper reviewed its original objective, stating: "There was no intention on the part of management to make the extensive search over a territory of possibly more than 10 square miles." In fact, the *Globe* claimed its sole object had been to prove conclusively that *Portland's* hull did not lie on, or inside Peaked Hill Bar. It concluded that Lieutenant Halpine and his party had absolutely determined this.

Four days later, Portland Steamship Company general manager John F. Liscomb and his Boston agent Charles Williams met with Lieutenant Halpine in a closed-door session at Halpine's office in the Boston Custom House. Following nearly two hours of discussion, Liscomb announced that he and Williams were leaving for New York, where they planned to meet "with interested persons with regard to instituting a search for the hull of the steamer *Portland*." The hastily arranged get-together was prompted by Liscomb's recent understanding that a "wealthy syndicate" had asked Halpine to lead another hunt for the steamship, "for the sole object of...pure gain." Liscomb was eager to forestall any such attempt until his company had made their own try.

Liscomb and the steamship company ultimately decided against any immediate plans to locate *Portland*, deciding to wait until more tranquil conditions the following spring and summer, which would facilitate the search. Halpine's investors put their plans on hold, as well.

In the meantime, the Canadian cable steamer *Minia* began the task of repairing the "Duxbury cable" in Massachusetts Bay. The telegraph link from Duxbury, Massachusetts, to maritime Canada had snapped the morning of November 27, near the great storm's height. After considerable testing, maintenance crews determined the submarine cable had broken at a point about seven miles east-northeast of Peaked Hill Bar, outside where the *Globe* expedition had looked. Many felt it possible—even hoped—that *Minia* might discover *Portland's* remains during the restoration work.

But *Minia* didn't find the wreck, and with the onset of wintry weather making further searches all but impossible the next several months, many people resigned themselves to the fact they might never know where *Portland* foundered. Early the following spring, however, the first in an ongoing series of "finds" rekindled the expectation.

On March 27, 1899, the fishing schooner *Maude S.*— one of the several vessels which reported sighting *Portland* off Cape Ann the night of its final trip—brought up scattered debris from a wreck in its trawls. The remnants con-

Some of the wreckage which came ashore at the time of *Portland's* foundering.

FOUR SHORT BLASTS

sisted of two electric-light brackets, a mattress, cabin furnishings, a heaving line, and a garter. Steamship agent Charles Williams positively identified the cabin objects as ones from the lost steamer *Portland*.

When he made the find, Captain William Thomas had been trawling off Stellwagen Bank. He told newspaper reporters he was 22 1/2 miles east-northeast of Boston Light, 17 miles southeast of Cape Ann, and 24 miles north-northwest of Highland Light, in water of 50 to 60 fathoms (300-360 feet). The spot was nearly atop where, a few weeks before, another fisherman had brought up some washbowl fittings that no one could positively identify.

Because of the water's depth, it would have been impossible for divers to explore the ocean floor where Captain Thomas had recovered the relics. At the time, 20 fathoms was as deep as any human had gone. Exploration of the site would have had to resort to grappling from the surface, and this was apparently never undertaken.

Over the next several years, other fishing vessels recovered a variety of objects from the floor of Massachusetts Bay, believed to have been from the missing steamer. A trawler brought up a brass lantern from a spot 12 miles southeast of Thacher's Island, near where Captain Pellier sighted *Portland* shortly after it was overtaken by the storm. In 1910, another vessel located one of the ship's chandeliers not far from the *Maude S.* finding. In April 1936, Captain Hayward Amirault, aboard the auxiliary dragger *Frances C. Denehy*, landed some plumbing fixtures pulled up some 30 miles southeast of Thacher's Island. At least one Boston newspaper report suggested that Captain

Amirault's discovery might have been from *Portland*, but because the spot is so much further offshore than any other known finds, that is highly unlikely.

On June 29, 1924, the scallop-dredger *Harriet Crie*, skippered by Captain Charles G. Carver of Rockland, Maine, landed in Plymouth with considerable debris he affirmed was from *Portland*. At the time, Carver was fishing in a newly opened scallop bed, approximately nine miles north of Highland Light. Among the items he recovered were an

Alice Rowe Snow, mother of Edward Rowe Snow, and an unidentified boy, holding a *Portland* life preserver from Snow's collection.

assortment of broken crockery, silverware, six champagne bottles, and a brass knob and lock from a stateroom door. One item which caused considerable speculation was a large iron stewpan bearing the letters "N E S Co." Several people suggested they stood for "New England Shipbuilding Company," the firm that constructed *Portland*. Carver said fellow draggers had found similar debris in the general area in recent days, and he expected others would bring up additional tangible evidence in the near future.

Lieutenant Halpine, who had led the *Boston Globe* search for the steamer a quarter century before, took exception to Carver's find. Questioned by a Boston newspaper reporter, Halpine stated, "I am still of the opinion that the wreck of the *Portland* lies outside of the Peaked Hill Bars somewhere, and I am equally confident that I can locate her and bring her into harbor, and I intend to do it, too."

Unlike Halpine, author Edward Rowe Snow felt Carver's find was the most credible evidence to date of *Portland's* final resting place. In 1944, Snow visited Captain Carver in Rockland, to hear more of the discovery firsthand. Snow later avowed that during the conversation, Carver claimed one of the recovered doorknobs bore the insignia of the Portland Steam Packet Company. And since *Portland* was the only vessel the company had lost anywhere near there, Carver felt certain it belonged to *Portland*.

According to Snow, Carver also gave him what he called "the exact location" of the 1924 find. Armed with this information and $1,800 of his own money, Snow sought out Malden diver Al George to find *Portland* for him. George worked the site during June and early July 1945 and after-

ward prepared and signed the following statement:

In the month of June 1945, I was commissioned by Lt. Edward R. Snow[1] to descend to the bottom of the ocean off Cape Cod at a location previously found by Captain Charles G. Carver of Rockland, Maine. Highland Light is at a distance of 4 1/2 miles; the Pilgrim Monument has a bearing of 210 degrees; Race Point Coast Guard Station is seven miles distant. Arriving on the location during the last week of June, I carried out the plans for finding the *Portland*. I ran a course 115 degrees true from the Peaked Hill Bar Buoy. I made a sweep after reaching a point 1 3/4 miles from the buoy, using a span of 600 feet of cable. We swept the entire location within a radius of three-quarters of a mile. On the second time across I made fast to what I knew was some large submerged object. After buoying it, we swept the entire vicinity to make sure the object was the steamer *Portland* and not some other wreck. Of this I am certain: This wreck is the only wreck in this vicinity which corresponds to the bearings given by Captain Carver. Therefore it must be the steamer *Portland*.

---

[1]Al George is referring here to Edward Rowe Snow's rank in the United States Air Force during World War II. A native of Massachusetts, Snow lived in Marshfield most of his life. The Islands of Boston Harbor, his first book, was derived from his graduate thesis at Harvard. For years, Snow attracted a large following across New England with his newspapers columns, radio shows, and more than 40 books about ghosts, shipwrecks and disasters; pirates and their buried treasure; and the unsolved mysteries of the sea. For many years at Christmas, he served as a flying Santa Claus, dropping gifts to the keepers of New England's lighthouses from a small plane. He died in 1982.

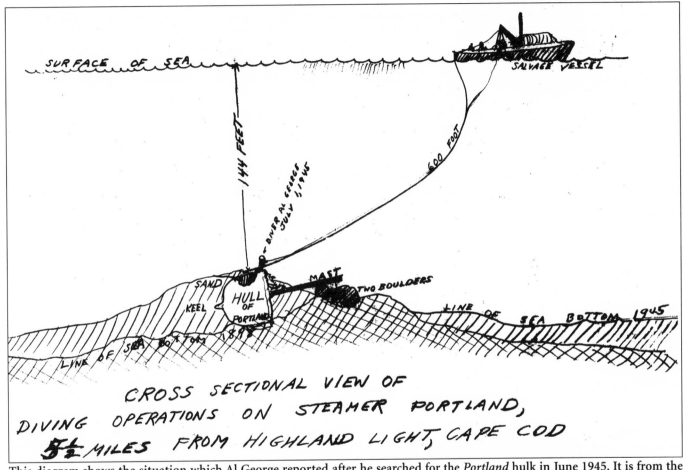

SURFACE OF SEA

SALVAGE VESSEL

144 FEET

600 FOOT

DIVER AL GEORGE JULY 1, 1945

SAND

KEEL

HULL OF PORTLAND

MAST

TWO BOULDERS

LINE OF SEA BOTTOM 1945

LINE OF SEA BOTTOM 1945

LINE OF SEA BOTTOM

CROSS SECTIONAL VIEW OF DIVING OPERATIONS ON STEAMER PORTLAND, 5½ MILES FROM HIGHLAND LIGHT, CAPE COD

This diagram shows the situation which Al George reported after he searched for the *Portland* hulk in June 1945. It is from the Edward Rowe Snow archive in the Department of Special Collections, Mugar Library, Boston University. Strangely, Snow never published it in any of his books, and it is not known if it was drawn by Snow, George, or an unknown third party.

Realizing this fact, I then got rigged for diving. I slid down the sweep wire and within three minutes of the time I had left the *Regavlas* I had landed on the *Portland,* which was over on its beam ends and heavily sanded in. It may surprise the average person to realize that the visibility here is less than 18 inches.

It was a weird sight. Crawling along the sloping hull of the vessel, I nosed my helmet forward until I ran into a mast heavily covered with marine growth (mussels, seaweed, etc.). Reaching my hands out, I found I could not span the mast. I followed the mast up until it went out of my reach at a space between two gigantic boulders on the bottom. The mast appeared to be broken off 15 feet up.

It would seem as though the *Portland* had hit bottom on her beam ends and then through the years had worked its way into the sand until it is buried almost completely. Only the bare hull of the ship seems in position.

All superstructure evidently has been spread around the ocean bed long ago. The boulders are much higher than my head. I could not tell whether it was the foremast or the mainmast. Going down on my hands and knees, I could make out the ripples of sand on the bottom of the sea and could see little shells from time to time.

The tide was running about one knot and it was slack water. My brother telephoned down from upstairs that he had 300 feet of line run out to enable me to stand on bottom in 144 feet of water.

It was a strange experience standing there alone with the ill-fated *Portland* and probably what remained of the passengers and crew still imprisoned in her sand-covered hull.

I wish I could give one the awesome picture. While visibility was a foot and a half, vague shadows could be made out up to five and eight feet away. Giant devil weed and long streamers of other varieties of seaweed shrouded me in a big black cloud of marine life.

As there will probably be many who might think that the *Portland* sank gently to the bottom to remain practically intact for the forty-seven years since the disaster, I must impress on their minds the true picture of the present conditions. The entire hull of the vessel which protrudes above the sand is a blackened shapeless mass of watersoaked wood, seaweed, mussels, scallops and scores of different types of marine growth.

I spent less than a half hour on the bottom, then I gave the signal to be hoisted up to twenty feet from the surface where I hung for ten minutes, then I was hoisted to ten feet from the surface where I remained for fifteen minutes. I was then brought over the side and my dive had been completed.

I realize that the purser's bell, the keys, the doorknobs and the many other articles which have been brought to the surface from this shipwreck indicate many more articles could be retrieved. I have been told that a small fortune in uncut gems in the purser's safe would well repay the lucky finder. In my opinion, however, although I would be happy to undertake the search, the chances are greatly against anything more of practical value ever being found. If anyone would consider financing such an enterprise, the cost would be prohibitive.

Al George

The Snow expedition to locate *Portland* settled the mat-

```
and stood on her deck--nearly a half centure after she
went down?

GEORGE:    Mighty weird Mr. Snow I can tell you, being down there
           alone at  the bottom of the sea, off Cape Cod--with as
           famous a shipwreck skeleton as the Portland, right in
           front of me. When you commissioned me to dive and locate
           the Portland--I never dared hope we'd be as successful as
           we were, in ending all the fabulous stories concerning her
           whereabouts.

SNOW:      Would you describe something of the Portland's position on
           the ocean floor, Al?

GEORGE:    Well, briefly, the Portland's better than three quarters
           submerged in the sand and mud. She's lying on her beams
           end--only the hull appears to remain. The super structure
           must be  spread all over the ocean--and there's one
           broken off mast--protruding from the hulk. I was somewhat
           in awe when I realized that the remains of the passengers
           and crew, whose bodies never came ashore--are probably
           still imprisoned in her sand covered hull.

SNOW:      And after having seen the Portland on the ocean floor---
           do you believe she must have been rammed and sunk by
           another ship during the storm?

GEORGE:    It's the only conclusion--well supported by fact, that can
           be drawn Mr. Snow. The Schooner Addie D. Snow, loaded
           with granite, blocks, must have crashed the Portland--
```

A page from the script of a radio interview of diver Al George conducted by Edward Rowe Snow for broadcast over WNAC in Boston. The program was one of many in whicheSnow told sea tales and interviewed a variety of interesting subjects about specific happenings in New England's maritime history.

ter for many. But for at least a few, there were still lingering doubts about what Al George had cryptically described, mixed with an unquenchable desire to know more. For them, the ultimate goal was to get conclusive proof of where the steamer lay—nothing less.

In the mid-1970s, members of the Historical Maritime Group of New England, a non-profit shipwreck research organization based in Bourne, Massachusetts, began its own active search for the steamship's remains. Using underwater magnetometers and side-scanning sonar, the outfit concentrated its efforts within a dozen miles of Provincetown. Although the scans resulted in several "hits," including the 1945 Snow site, they failed to show anything "even close to the *Portland,*" according to H. Arnold Carr, one of HMG's founders. Commenting on the wreckage Al George described in his statement to Snow, Carr speculated it "could have been debris from the *Portland,*" but he refused to believe it was the actual ship.

After several unsuccessful seasons of hunting, HMG expanded its search further north, relying on computer-generated feedback from Richard Limeburner, a physical oceanographer at the Woods Hole Oceanographic Institute. Limeburner carried out a lengthy drift analysis, based on contemporary weather and tide data. Following several months of work, Limeburner narrowed the proposed search site to a few square miles. The general area had long been popular with fishermen working the Middle Bank, midway between Cape Ann and Cape Cod. During 1988, at a spot where many boats had snagged nets and trawls, HMG's sonar showed what its operators identified as a large wreck that fit the characteristics of the sought-after steamship. Unable to investigate further due to prior commitments, Carr and colleagues John Perry Fish and William McElroy waited until the following spring to return.

In April 1989, the group made a significant find. Probing the site with a "sediment sampler," they hauled up what Fish described as parts of a ship's rigging, coal from the engine area, and some of the ship's timbers. They also obtained images which they described as showing a hull that had been split lengthwise. According to John Fish, "We found something that appeared to have exploded."

After carefully evaluating the evidence, HMG went public with the discovery. The group held a news conference in Boston, during which they tentatively identified the hulk they had found as that of *Portland*. The wreck hunters also released images they asserted as showing the stern section of the ship. One purportedly depicted an engine component; another, one of the chocks, a heavy, curved metal fitting through which mooring lines passed.

Carr, Fish, and McElroy also announced their intention to revisit the wreck site, roughly 20 miles north of Provincetown, as soon as they could. Because the remains were so deep—between 300 and 400 feet—the men would be unable to dive to it with conventional gear. Instead, they hoped to obtain the use of a research submarine, but if that were not possible they would employ underwater photography and a remote-controlled vehicle. In this fashion, they planned to ultimately obtain the irrefutable proof—something displaying the steamship's name, the company's logo, or perhaps the engine or boiler numbers—that the

Edward Rowe Snow and the Portland Associates placed this plaque on Highland Light in 1956 to mark the loss of the *Portland*

wreck was *Portland*. HMG's endeavors are ongoing.

Aside from the efforts of those attempting to locate *Portland's* physical remains, others have nurtured the steamer's legacy in more personal terms. In 1908, relatives and friends of those lost when the ship sank, created an affiliation called the *Portland* Associates. It became the group's custom to hold annual memorial services at India Wharf, Boston, from where the steamer sailed its final night. At 7:00 p.m. each November 26, one of the members would read aloud the victims' names. At the conclusion of the list, another would drop flowers into the harbor waters. Afterward, those gathered would exchange reminiscences of the tragic weekend and share personal

Edward Rowe Snow and a group of *Portland* Associates members display a banner bearing the name *Portland* following a memorial service conducted on Portland's Custom House Wharf in the late 1970's

Edward Rowe Snow and Marie Hansen, Sons and Daughters of the *Portland* Associates president, with a painting of *Portland*.

conjecture regarding the ship's—and their loved ones'—final, nightmarish hours.

On the 50th anniversary of the sinking, November 26, 1948, the *Portland* Associates agreed it would be their final get-together. Led by then-president John A. Thornquist of Medford, Massachusetts, 80 of the faithful congregated on India Wharf for concluding prayers and ceremonies.

Eight years later, a smaller group conducted by Edward Rowe Snow met at Highland Light, where Snow unveiled a bronze plaque, fastened to the light tower, to commemorate the *Portland* victims.

More recently, the Sons and Daughters of the *Portland* Associates carried on the annual memorial tradition in Boston. Into the 1970s, members of the group also made an annual pilgrimage to Maine, for similar ceremonies on the Portland waterfront. Beginning in 1956, Miss Marie Hansen of Cambridge, Massachusetts, served as the group's president, receiving considerable support and assistance from Snow.

Through the middle years of the twentieth century, Edward Rowe Snow actively kept alive the *Portland* story, recounting the disaster in several of his dozens of books chronicling New England's rich coastal heritage and via lectures and radio broadcasts throughout the six-state area. During the 1940s, he narrated a weekly radio show entitled *Six Bells*, over Boston radio station WNAC. The Sunday afternoon broadcasts, sponsored by the H.P. Hood Company, featured half-hour reenactments of various historic events of interest along New England shores. The December 2, 1945, presentation was entitled "The Mystery of the Steamer *Portland*" and delivered a highly dramatic re-creation of a fanciful account—complete with howling winds, hammering noises, engine sounds, horns, bells, creaks and groans, etc.—of the vessel's last voyage. The steamer's imagined, final moments are played out in the following brief excerpts, drawn from the actual script, between Captain Hollis Blanchard and Second Mate John McKay:

Blanchard: (Grunting) Hold her, McKay - - that wheel gets away from us once and we're broadside - - we'll be finished - - - ! If this keeps up much longer, it'll be hopeless - - we're shipping lots of water through our wheel guards and open seams!

Shortly thereafter...

McKay: (Stark Terror) My God! - - - Captain! Look there on the starboard quarter - - - - a ship bearing down!!

Blanchard: (Horrified) A schooner! On top of us! She's going to ram us, McKay! Hard a-port! Hard a-port!!

The stirring presentation fired the imaginations of countless listeners. Some were old enough to have learned the tragic news first-hand, nearly a half century before. To most, however, it was history come alive, especially ones hearing the gripping tale for the first time.

The salvaged remains of the steamer *Portland* have contributed to keeping alive the ship's legacy, as well. In the hours following the disaster, several Cape Cod residents picked up various pieces of *Portland's* wreckage from the beaches where it had piled up on the shore. F.E. Chamberlain of Wellfleet rescued a red upholstered chair with mahogany frame, as well as a part of the ship's piano. Charles Ayling of Centerville recovered one of *Portland's* wheels; Captain Rufus Snow, another. Captain Daniel Gould of Orleans gathered up as many as a bushel of keys.

Cy Young, who operated an antique shop in Provincetown, filled his wagon with whatever he could secure—doors, cabin posts, life belts, bottles of rum, even some empty coffins—which he stored and sold for nearly a half century afterward. Edward Rowe Snow purchased two of the doors in 1942 and had them cut into tiny slivers, which

he inserted into copies of one of his later books.

Several vestiges of *Portland's* remains have been handed down through the generations. The majority repose in private hands, as treasured family heirlooms or in exclusive collections. Others eventually found their way into museums and similar archives, where the public may view them today. The Pilgrim Monument & Provincetown Museum displays one of the vessel's life jackets, an oar stenciled with the words "Str. *Portland*," a champagne glass, a brass baggage check bearing the number "711," and the ceramic plaque that designated

Captain Rufus Snow of Orleans with a ship's wheel which washed ashore after the *Portland* foundered.

This rare stained glass window of the *Portland* hangs in a home on the Maine coast.

stateroom 169.[2] The Maine Maritime Museum in Bath has the ship's engine room gong and another oar.

At the Truro Historical Museum, near Highland Light, are three *Portland* chairs—one a Brentwood, with burgundy plush covering, and another with a wicker seat; two 8-oz. drinking glasses; an ornate door escutcheon; and a book of Whittier's poems, which may have belonged to one of the passengers. The group's "prized possession," in the words of society president Bruce Tarvers, is what he believes is *Portland's* stern post, which was given to the museum by Captain Joseph Roderick, a longtime Provincetown fisherman.

Captain Roderick brought up the heavy wooden stock, used to support the ship's rudder, in the late 1950s. He had been fishing from the dragger *Jimmy Boy* on what he called the "scallop ground," a popular area along the south side of Stellwagen Bank, seven or eight miles north-northeast of Race Point. The once burly timber, which he pulled from "about 27 or 28 fathoms" (162-168 feet), stands more than six feet high. It has been substantially eaten by marine worms, but retains its heavy bronze fixtures and is still an impressive piece. Captain Joe, now 76, fished out of Provincetown from 1939 through 1987, and remembered that over the years, he and his crew fished up numerous other pieces of wreckage which they could never identify as coming from the *Portland* or from another wreck.[3]

Today, as then, the *Portland* saga continues to captivate New Englanders and students of maritime history, far and wide. During the intervening century, many have tried to solve the mysteries surrounding the vessel's disappearance and loss. While some have produced evidence that partially lifts the veil of secrecy, the final story in all its lurid detail has yet to be told. With few exceptions, these specifics will forever remain a secret.

Regardless of what else may come to light, the unfortunate loss of the steamer *Portland* and the lives of the nearly 200 men, women, and children with it was a shocking occurrence. It will remain one of the greatest maritime disasters— and mysteries—in New England history.

Left: The Truro Historical Society proudly displays this maritime relic which it believes is a portion of the *Portland's* sternpost.

[2] During 1998, the museum displayed the objects in a special exhibition *Storms and Shipwrecks of the Outer Cape.* Included in the exhibition was the original of the cover painting of this book, painted by Roland Borduas of Portland, Maine.

[3] Captain Roderick, in a special inteview for this book, told the authors that over the years he and his crew had hauled up numerous pieces of wreckage which they could not identify, and he had often wished he could know more about what he had pulled from the bottom.

Victims of *Portland* Sinking — November 27, 1898
PASSENGERS

Name	*Hometown*		
1. *Allen, Frederick H.*	Buxton or Scarborough, ME	33. Foden, Robert	Portland, ME
2. *Atamian, George*	Portland, ME	34. Fowler, Frederick	East Deering, ME
3. Baker, Beulah Mosely	Portland, ME	35. *Freeman, Elias Dudley*	Yarmouth, ME
4. Beardsworth, William	South Portland, ME	36. Frye, Isaiah	Portland, ME
5. *Bemis, Cora Vosmus* [S]	Auburn, ME	37. Frye, Miss Ruth	Portland, ME
6. Bemis, Walter L.	Auburn, ME	38. Galley, John G.	Portland, ME
7. Bonney, George Alonzo	Portland, ME	39. Gatchell, Dennis Osborne	Boston, MA
8. Briggs, Mr.	New York, NY	40. Gatley, Mrs. Ellen Driscoll	Portland, ME
9. *Brown, Fred A.*	Portland, ME	41. Gibson, George P.	Windsor, NS
10. Buckminster, Vernley	East Providence, RI	42. *Goggin, A.A.*	Marlboro, MA
11. Carroll, Mrs. J.A.	Portland, ME	43. *Gosselin, Alphonse*	Montreal, PQ, Canada
12. Chase, Philip Adams [C]	Worcester, MA	44. Hanley, Matthew	Reading, MA
13. Chase, William Livingston	Worcester, MA	45. Hanson, William	Gorham, ME
14. *Chickering, Abbie C.*	Weymouth, MA	46. Heald, Miss Rowena M.	Cumberland Mills, ME
15. Clark, Albert	Somerville, MA	47. Hersom, Arthur F.	Portland, ME
16. Cobb, Miss Emily L.	Portland, ME	48. Hersom, Mrs. Arthur F.	Portland, ME
17. *Cohen, Solomon*	Portland, ME	49. *Holmes, Miss Sophie B.*	Portland, ME
18. Cole, George W.	South Portland, ME	50. Hooper, Carl [C]	Portland, ME
19. *Collins, Miss Elizabeth M.A.*	Portland, ME	51. *Hooper, Oren*	Portland, ME
20. *Cottreau, Charles C.*	Yarmouth, NS	52. Hoyt, Miss Cynthia Jennie	North Easton, MA
21. Curtis, Miss Elizabeth	Lisbon, ME	53. *Ingraham, Miss Madge*	Woodfords, ME
22. Daly, Jerry	Portland, ME	54. Jackson, Lillian [S]	South Portland, ME
23. *Delaney, George Edward*	Boston, MA	55. Jackson, Malcolm [C]	South Portland, ME
24. Dennis, Mrs. Ezekiel	Portland, ME	56. Jackson, Perry	South Portland, ME
25. Doherty, John	Boston, MA	57. *Kelley, Miss Susan Annie*	Dorchester, MA
26. *Dunbar, Burke*	Penobscot, ME	58. Kennedy, William	Buxton or Scarborough, ME
27. Dwyer, W.Y.	Portland, ME	59. Kenniston, George B., Jr.	Boothbay, ME
28. Dyer, N.J.	Portland, ME	60. *Kinyon, Miss Florence Muriel*	Cambridge, MA
29. *Edmonds, Mrs. Jennie G.*	East Boston, MA	61. Kirby, Timothy	Marlboro, MA
30. Edwards, Lawrence	North Abington, MA	62. Langthorne, Miss Helen M.	Deering, ME
31. Flower, James W.	Lewiston, ME	63. Leighton, Diane Gilbert [S]	Portland, ME
32. Foden, Rachel [S]	Portland, ME	64. Leighton, Ora L.	Portland, ME

[S] indicates a spouse traveling with her husband; [C] means a child traveling with a family member.
A name in *the italic* face indicates the person's body was found.

Appendix One

65.	Lord, Mrs. Hattie A.	East Deering, ME
66.	*Mann, John G.*	Portland, ME
67.	Matthews, child [c]	Freeport, ME
68.	Matthews, Mr. Albert	Freeport, ME
69.	Matthews, Mrs. Albert [s]	Freeport, ME
70.	McGilverney, D.W.	Roxbury, MA
71.	McGowan, Miss Lilla	Portland, ME
72.	McKenney, Mrs.	South Portland, ME
73.	McMullen, Miss Jennie G.	Portland, ME
74.	*Metcalf, Lewis J.*	Brockton, MA
75.	*Mitchell, Mrs. Cornelia N.*	North Easton, MA
76.	Morong, Miss Faith	Portland, ME
77.	*Mosher, Willard J.*	Gorham, ME
78.	Munn, William Frederick	Suffield, CT
79.	Murphy, John H.	Portland, ME
80.	Murphy, John J.	Marlboro, MA
81.	O'Connell, John	Portland, ME
82.	*Piche, Jules Procul*	Montreal, PQ, Canada
83.	*Plympton, Miss Emma L.*	Charles River, MA
84.	Pratt, Miss Amy [c]	Portland, ME
85.	Pratt, Mrs. Horace	Portland, ME
86.	Prescott, George Luther	Berlin, NH
87.	*Proctor, Warren Scott*	South Portland, ME
88.	Ravenelle, Theodore	Lowell, MA
89.	Reynolds, Miss Alice	Portland, ME
90.	Richardson, Frank F.	Cambridge, MA
91.	Roche, William Henry	Portland, ME
92.	Roddy, James	Everett, MA
93.	Safford, Mrs. Miranda	Portland, ME
94.	Schmidt, Anton [c]	Deering, ME
95.	Schmidt, Jes Jessen	Deering, ME
96.	Schmidt, Jessine [s]	Deering, ME
97.	Schmidt, Jorgen Jessen [c]	Portland, ME
98.	Sherwood, Fred	Portland, ME
99.	Silverstaine, Harry [c]	Portland, ME
100.	Silverstaine, Louis	Portland, ME
101.	Small, Merton L.	Portland, ME
102.	Smith, Harry	East Boston, MA
103.	Stanley, James	Brooklin, ME
104.	Sullivan, Mrs. John	Portland, ME
105.	Swift, Miss Ella	Portland,ME
106.	Sykes, Miss Maude	Portland, ME
107.	Tetrow, Miss Annie	Manchester, NH
108.	Thompson, Charles H.	Portland, ME
109.	Thompson, Gladys M. [c]	Portland, ME
110.	Thompson, Susan E. [s]	Portland, ME
111.	Tibbetts, Charles A.	So. Portland, ME
112.	Timmons, Mrs. Almira	Malden, MA
113.	*Tinkham, Charles A.*	Hartford, CT
114.	*Totten, Miss Eva*	Cambridge, MA
115.	Tucker, Miss Alice	Lowell, MA
116.	Tupper, James	Brunswick, ME
117.	Turner, Augustus, R.	Auburn, ME
118.	Turner, Mrs. Augustus R.	Auburn, ME
119.	Twombly, Mrs.	Bangor, ME
120.	VanGuysling, C.E.	Albany, NY
121.	Welsh, Mary	Unknown
122.	*Wheeler, Eunice Augusta*	South Weymouth, MA
123.	White, Horace	Scarborough, ME
124.	Wiggin, Charles	Portland, ME
125.	Wildes, Alonzo F.	Bath, M
126.	Wilson, Frank	St. John, NB, Canada
127.	Young, Harry de Merritt	Auburndale, MA

Name	Position	Hometown
1. Allen, Henry George	porter	Boston, MA
2. Barron, Matthew	deck crew	
3. Berry, Mrs. Margaret	stewardess	Portland, ME
4. Blake, Rodney	watchman	Portland, ME
5. Blanchard, Hollis Henry	captain	East Deering, ME
6. Bruce, D.	deck crew	
7. Carter, Allan	fireman	Brockton, MA
8. Cash, William H.	saloonman	Boston, MA
9. Clayton, Harry		Boston, MA
10. *Collins, Peter*	deck crew	Hanover, MA
11. Cropley, George H.	deck crew	So. Portland, ME
12. Crozier, John	deck crew	
13. Daley, John H.	deck crew	
14. Dauplimais, Edward	deck crew	Northampton, MA
15. Davidson, James (or Joseph)	deck crew	
16. Dennett, William	deck crew	
17. *Dillon, John Albert*	oiler	
18. Doughty, William J.	fireman	
19. Dyer, Ansel L.	quartermaster	Portland, ME
20. Foreman, Lee	saloonman	
21. Gately, John K.	fireman	Portland, ME
22. Gatlin, Alexander	saloonman	
23. *Graham, George*	cabinman	
24. Graham, Morris	deck crew	
25. Hamilton, Charles	deck crew	
26. Harris, Mrs. Carrie E. M.	stewardess	
27. Hartley, Richard	deck crew	
28. Hemmingway, William Alex	cabinman	Boston, MA
29. Heuston, Francis Eben	sec. steward	Portland, ME
30. Howard, Stephen	first cook	Boston, MA
31. Ingraham, Frederick A.	purser	Portland, ME
32. Johnston, Arthur E.	sal. watchman	Portland, ME
33. *Jones, John F.*	acting third cook	

Name	Position	Hometown
34. Latttimer, William	head saloonman	Boston, MA
35. Leighton, Frank W.	electrician	
36. MacGilvray, George T.	deck crew	Roxbury, MA
37. Mackey, John	second mate	So. Portland, M
38. Mathews, Alonzo V.	first steward	Cambridge, MA
39. McNeil, James	oiler	Portland, ME
40. Menott, Michael	saloonman	
41. Merrill, Thomas B.	first engineer	Portland, ME
42. Merriman, Hugh	fireman	So. Portland, ME
43. Mondary, Thomas	saloon watchman	
44. Moore, Horace	clerk	Portland, ME
45. *Mundrucen, Theodore*	steward	Cambridge, MA
46. Nelson, Lewis	second pilot	Portland, ME
47. Norton, George A.	deck crew	Fitchburg, MA
48. O'Brien, Cornelius	deck crew	
49. Oxley (or Oxby), Ernest	pantryman	
50. Patterson, Frank A.	quartermaster	
51. *Pennell, Thomas H.*	fireman	Boston, MA
52. Penuckle, Henry	saloonman	
53. *Pina, Jerome J.*	cabinman	
54. Reed, Griffin S.	forward cabin watch	
55. Winthrop B. Robicheau	baggage master	Portland, ME
56. Rollister, Harry	fireman	Portland, ME
57. Sewall, Thomas	watchman	Portland, ME
58. Sloan, Arthur	deck crewman	
59. *Smith, Samuel H.*	saloonman	
60. Thompson, George A.	cabinman	
61. Verrill, Charles E.	third engineer	Portland, ME
62. *Walton, John T.*	second engineer	Portland, ME
63. Wells (or Will), Fred	third cook	Portland, ME
64. Whitten, John C.	watchman	Portland, ME
65. Williams, James	watchman	Boston, MA

Appendix One

List of Vessels Lost or Damaged in the Great November 1898 Gale

Type	Name	Cause	Location	Lives lost
Sch	*A.B. Nickerson*		Provincetown, MA	
Sch	*A.C. White*	stranded	Spectacle Is., Boston Harbor, MA	
Sch	*Abbie Morrisey*	wrecked	Rocky Neck Cove, Gloucester, MA	
Sch	*Abby K.. Bentley*	stranded	Vineyard Haven, MA	
Sch	*Abel E. Babcock*	stranded	Toddy Rocks, Hull, MA	8
Sch	*Addie E. Snow*	foundered	off Provincetown, MA	6
Sch	*Addie Sawyer*		Vineyard Haven, MA	3
Slp	*Adalaide T.*		Hither Plain, NY	
	Africa	stranded	Portland, ME	
Sch	*Agnes*	stranded	Provincetown Harbor, MA	
Sch	*Agnes May*	stranded	Salem Harbor, MA	
Sch	*Agnes Smith*	stranded	Point Judith, RI	
Sch	*Albert H. Harding*	stranded	Boston Harbor, MA	
Sch	*Albert L. Butler*	wrecked	Provincetown, MA	3
Y	*Alice*	foundered	off Ten Pound Island, Gloucester, MA	
Sch	*Alida*		Islesboro, ME	
Sch	*Aloha*		Block Island, RI	
Sch y	*Alsation*	foundered	Port Jefferson, L.I., NY	
Sch	*Amelia Ireland*	wrecked	off Gay Head, Marthas Vineyard, MA	1
Sch	*Amy Knight*	stranded	White Is., off Vinalhaven Island, ME	
Sch	*Anna H. Mason*	wrecked	Eastern Point, Gloucester, MA	
Slp	*Anna Pitcher*		Block Island, RI	
Sch	*Anna W. Barker*		Southern Is., Tenants Harbor, ME	
Sch	*Annie Lee*		Pigeon Cove, Rockport, MA	
Sch	*Annie Louise*	stranded	Provincetown, MA	
Sch	*Arabell*		Block Island, RI	
Bge	*Aragon*	foundered	off Halifax, NS	6
Bge	*Atlantic*	foundered	Newburyport, MA	
Sch	*Avalon*	wrecked	off Cape Cod, MA	
Bge	*Balloon*		New Bedford, MA	
Bge	*Beaver*		New Bedford, MA	
Sch	*Belle Franklin*	stranded	Smith's Cove, Gloucester, MA	

Key — Vessel Types

Bge=barge; Bk=bark; Bkn=barkentine; Brig=brig; Cat=cat; Lch=launch; Ltr=lighter; Sch=schooner; Sch y=schooner yacht; Slp=sloop; Slp y=sloop yacht; Smk=smack; St l=steam lighter; St p=steamship; St s=steam screw; Tug=tug; Y=yacht

Sch	*Bertha E. Glover*	stranded	Vineyard Haven, MA	
Sch	*Bessie H. Gross*	stranded	House Island, Manchester., MA	3
Bge	*Bingham*	foundered	Long Island Sound, NY	
Sch	*Blanche M. Thorbourne*	stranded	Liverpool Harbor, NS	
Bge	*Bravo*	foundered	Vineyard Haven, MA	
Sch y	*Brunhilde*		Point of Woods, NY	
Bge	*Budget*		Vineyard Haven, MA	
Ltr	*Burnham*	ashore	Rainsford Island, Boston Harbor, MA	
Bge	*Byssus*	foundered	Vineyard Haven, MA	
Sch	*C.A. White*	stranded	Spectacle Is., Boston Harbor, MA	
Sch	*Calvin F. Baker*	foundered	off Little Brewster Is., Boston, MA	3
Sch	*Canaria*	stranded	Vineyard Haven, MA	
Sch	*Carita*	stranded	Vineyard Haven, MA	
Sch	*Carrie C. Miles*	dismasted	off Peaks Island, Portland, ME	
Slp	*Carrie E.*	wrecked	Lubec, ME	
Sch	*Carrie E. Sayward*	stranded	Wood End, Provincetown, MA	
Sch	*Carrie F. Roberts*	stranded	Rocky Neck Cove, Gloucester, MA	
Slp	*Carrie Lida*		Provincetown, MA	
Slp	*Cassia*	wrecked	off Block Island, RI	1
Sch	*Catharine*	collision	Hyannis, MA	
Sch	*Cathie C. Berry*	ashore	Vineyard Haven, MA	
Y	*Cavalier*	stranded	Rocky Neck Cove, Gloucester, MA	
St y	*Chaffee*	foundered	Pigeon Cove, Rockport, MA	
Sch	*Champion*		Provincetown, MA	
Brig	*Champion*	wrecked	Lubec, ME	
Sch	*Charles Caswell*	stranded	Plymouth, MA	
Sch	*Charles E. Raymond*		Vineyard Haven, MA	
Sch	*Charles E. Schmidt*	stranded	Knowlton's Point, Rockport, MA	
Sch	*Charles J. Willard*	stranded	Lubec, ME	
Sch	*Charles W. Parker*	stranded	off Plymouth, MA	
Sch	*Chilion*	stranded	Rockport, MA	
Sch	*Chiswick*	wrecked	Scituate, MA	
Sch	*Christina Moore*	stranded	Vineyard Haven, MA	
Slp	*City of Everett*	stranded	Rocky Neck Breakwater, Gloucester, MA	
Sch	*Clara*	stranded	Provincetown, MA	
Sch	*Clara B. Kennard*	stranded	Fort Point, Boston Harbor, MA	

Appendix Two

Sch	*Clara C. Baker	wrecked	off Marthas Vineyard, MA	
Sch	Clara J. Given		Provincetown, MA	
Sch	Clara Leavitt	wrecked	Marthas Vineyard, MA	6
Sch	Clara P. Sewall	stranded	Plymouth, MA	
Sch	Clara Sayward		Provincetown, MA	
Sch	Columbia	stranded	Scituate Beach, MA	5
Bge	Corsica	foundered	off Sandy Hook, NJ	4
Sch	D.K. Baker	foundered	off NJ coast	
Sch	D.T. Pachin		Gloucester, MA	
Sch	Daniel Boone		Provincetown, MA	
Sch	Daniel I. Tenney	stranded	off Sandy Neck, Barnstable, MA	6
Smk	Daphne		Provincetown, MA	
Sch	David Faust		Nantucket, MA	
Bge	Delaware	foundered	off Egypt Beach, Cohasset, MA	6
Sch	Dewitt	stranded	Salem Harbor, MA	
Slp	Donum	wrecked	Paddocks Island, Boston Harbor, MA	
Sch	E.G. Willard	stranded	Canal Flats, Vineyard Haven, MA	
Sch	E.J. Hamilton	wrecked	Vineyard Haven, MA	
Bge	E.W. Stetson	stranded	Minor Hill, L.I., NY	
Cat	Earl	stranded	Cuttyhunk, MA	
Sch	Eddie A. Minot	stranded	Marblehead, MA	
Sch	Edgar S. Foster	wrecked	Brant Rock Shoals, Marshfield, MA	8
Cat	Edith	stranded	Cuttyhunk, MA	
Sch	Edith McIntyre		Vineyard Haven, MA	
Sch	Edward H. Smeed		Block Island, RI	
Sch	Effie F. Morrissey	stranded	Smith's Cove, Gloucester, MA	
Sch	Eldora	ashore	Cape Porpoise, Kennebunkport, ME	
Slp	Ella		Provincetown, MA	
Sch	Ella F. Crowell	wrecked	Veazie's Rock, Quincy, MA	
Sch	Ella Francis		Provincetown, MA	
Sch	Ellen Jones		Provincetown, MA	
Sch	Ellis P. Rogers	stranded	Forest River, Salem Harbor, MA	
Sch	Elmer E. Randall		Plymouth, MA	
Smk	Elwyn		Provincetown, MA	
Sch	Emma	foundered	off Sandy Neck, Barnstable, MA	3
Sch	Emma M. Dyer	wrecked	off Highland Light, Cape Cod, MA	

Sch	*Ernst T. Lee*	collision	Vineyard Haven, MA	
Bge	*Escort*	wrecked	Horton's Point, Port Jefferson, L.I., NY	3
Sch	*Ethel F. Merriam*	stranded	Gloucester Harbor, MA	
Y	*Eulisie*	stranded	Rocky Neck, Gloucester, MA	
Sch	*Evelyn*	stranded	Salem Harbor, MA	
Sch	*Everett*	foundered	off Shelter Is., Greenport, L.I., NY	
Sch	*F.H. Smith*		Provincetown, MA	
Sch	*F.P. Foster*		Provincetown, MA	
Sch	*F.R. Walker*	foundered	off Race Point, Provincetown, MA	14
Stm s	*Fairfax*	stranded	Sow and Pigs Shoals, Cuttyhunk, MA	
Stm bge	*Falcon*	foundered	Vineyard Haven, MA	
Sch	*Fannie F. Hall*		Portsmouth, NH	
Slp	*Fannie May*		Rockland, ME	
Slp	*Ferguson*		New London, CT	
Sch	*Fitz A. Oakes*	stranded	Plymouth, MA	
Sch	*Flora Condon*	ashore	Vineyard Haven, MA	
Sch	*Florence I. Lockwood*	foundered	off Cape Cod, MA	10
Sch	*Flying Cloud*	foundered	off Marblehead Neck, MA	
Sch	*Forest Maid*		Portsmouth, NH	
Sch	*Forest Queen*	wrecked	Fort Point, Stockton Springs, ME	
Slp	*Francis*		Provincetown Harbor, MA	
Sch	*Frank*	wrecked	Ten Pound Island, Gloucester, MA	
Sch	*Frank Foster*	stranded	Provincetown, MA	
Sch	*Frank H. Smith*	stranded	Provincetown, MA	
Sch	*Fred A. Emerson*	stranded	Thompson's Is., Boston Harbor, MA	
Sch	*Freddie W. Alton*	stranded	Moon Is., Boston Harbor, MA	
Sch	*Freedom*	stranded	Plymouth, MA	
Smk	*Freeman*		Provincetown, MA	
St s	*Friend*	collision	Cuttyhunk, MA	
Sch	*G.M. Hopkins*	wrecked	off Ft. Warren, Boston Harbor, MA	
St s	*G.W. Danielson*		Block Island, RI	
Sch	*G.W. Rawley*		Edgartown, Marthas Vineyard, MA	
Sch	*Gatherer*		Pigeon Cove, Rockport, MA	
St s	*George A. Chaffee*	wrecked	Pigeon Cove, Rockport, MA	
Sch	*George A. Pierce*	collision	Vineyard Haven, MA	
Sch	*George H. Mills*	stranded	Canal Flats, Vineyard Haven, MA	

Appendix Two

Sch	*Georgietta*		Spruce Head, ME	
Slp	*Gracie*	stranded	off Wood End LSS, Cape Cod, MA	3
Bge	*Grant*	stranded	Gallop's Island, Boston Harbor, MA	
Sch	*H.A. Hawgood*	stranded	Boston Harbor, MA	
St y	*Halcyon*	foundered	Port Jefferson, L.I., NY	
Slp	*Hard Chance*	stranded	Port Jefferson, L.I., NY	4
Sch	*Harriet M. Young*		Provincetown, MA	
Sch	*Hattie A. Butler*	ashore	Buzzards Bay, MA	1
Sch	*Hattie Douglass*		New London, CT	
Sch	*Hattie M. Howes*		Vineyard Haven, MA	
Bge	*Haverford*	stranded	Boston Harbor, MA	
Sch	*Hector*		Vineyard Haven, MA	
Slp	*Helena*	stranded	Rocky Neck Cove, Gloucester, MA	
Bge	*Helicon*	foundered	off Barnegat light, Long Beach, NJ	4
Sch	*Henrietta Simmons*	collision	Vineyard Haven, MA	
Sch	*Henry R. Tilton*	stranded	Toddy Rocks, Hull, MA	
St l	*Hero*	wrecked	North River, Salem, MA	
Y	*Hoodoo*	stranded	Rocky Neck, Gloucester, MA	
Sch	*Hume*		Boston Harbor, MA	
St s	*Hurricane*		Rockland, ME	
Sch	*I.A. Hamlin*		Block Island, RI	
Sch y	*Ida*		Plymouth Harbor, MA	
Cat	*Ida G. Broere*		Lone Hill, NY	
Sch	*Idella Small*	stranded	Ipswich, MA	
Sch	*Inez Hatch*		Provincetown, MA	
St l	*Institution*		Boston Harbor, MA	
Sch	*Ira and Abbie*		Point Judith, RI	
Sch	*Ira Kilburn*		Portsmouth, NH	
Bge	*Iron City*	stranded	Boston Harbor, MA	
Sch	*Isaac Collins*		Provincetown, MA	
Sch	*Island City*		Cottage City, Vineyard Haven, MA	5
Sch	*Ivy Belle*	stranded	Odiorne's Point, N H	
Sch	*J.C. Mahoney*	wrecked	near Naugus Head, Marblehead, MA	
Sch	*J.D. Ingraham*	wrecked	Vineyard Haven, MA	
Sch	*J.J. Little*	stranded	Plymouth, MA	
Sch	*J.K. Manning*	stranded	Gloucester, MA	

Appendix Two

Sch	*J.M. Eaton*		Cape Ann, MA	
Sch	*James A. Brown*	wrecked	Vineyard Haven, MA	
Sch	*James A. Stetson*	foundered	Pigeon Cove Harbor, Rockport, MA	
Sch	*James A. Webster*	stranded	off Lawley's Basin, Boston Harbor, MA	
Sch	*James Drinan*	wrecked	Rocky Neck Cove, Gloucester, MA	
Sch	*James H. Hoyt*		off Nantasket Beach, Hull, MA	
Sch	*James Ponder*		Vineyard Haven, MA	
Slp	*Jennie*		Elizabeth Islands, MA	
Sch	*John Corbal*	stranded	off Thompson's Is., Boston Harbor, MA	
Brig	*John Garvey*		Point Judith, RI	
St s	*John J. Hill*	stranded	Wollaston Beach, Quincy, MA	
Sch	*John S. Ames*	stranded	Georges Island, Boston Harbor, MA	
Sch	*Jordan L. Mott*	stranded	Provincetown, MA	1
Sch	*Julia A. Decker*	stranded	Plum Island, MA	
Sch	*Juniata*	wrecked	Beach Island, Cohasset, MA	
Sch y	*Kathleen*	wrecked	Hingham, MA	
Sch	*King Philip*	foundered	off Provincetown, MA	13
Sch y	*Kittie*		Saybrook, NY	
Sch	*Knott V. Martin*	foundered	Marblehead Harbor, MA	
Sch	*Leander V. Beebe*	wrecked	Black Rock, Cohasset, MA	9
S ch	*Lena White*	stranded	Prudence Island, RI	
Sch	*Leora M. Thurlow*	foundered	Vineyard Haven, MA	1
Sch	*Lester A. Lewis*	stranded	Provincetown, MA	5
Sch	*Letha May*		Provincetown, MA	
Sch	*Levuka*	wrecked	Forest Cove, Perry, ME	
Sch	*Lexington*	wrecked	Block Island, RI	
Smk	*Lila*	stranded	Provincetown, MA	
Sch	*Lillian*		Portland, ME	
Sch	*Lizzie Dyas*	stranded	Georges Island, Boston Harbor, MA	
Sch	*Lizzie Lee*	wrecked	Moon Island, Boston Harbor, MA	
Y	*Lotus*	foundered	off Rocky Neck, Gloucester, MA	
Bk	*Lucy A. Nickels*	wrecked	Gun Rock, Cohasset, MA	3
Sch	*Lucy Belle*	stranded	foot of Swett St., Boston Harbor, MA	
Sch	*Lucy Eldridge*	overturned	Nantucket, MA	
Sch	*Lucy Hammond*	stranded	Vineyard Haven, MA	
Sch	*Lunet*	stranded	Tarpaulin Cove, Naushon Island, RI	7

Sch	*M.B. Mahoney*	stranded	Saugus Head, Salem Harbor, MA	
Sch	*M.E. Eldridge*	stranded	Vineyard Haven, MA	
Bge	*Macauley*	wrecked	Boston Harbor, MA	
Sch	*Maggie Ellen*		New London, CT	
Tug	*Margaret J. Sanford*	stranded	Sand Point, Prudence Island, RI	
Sch	*Marguerite*	stranded	Smith's Cove, Gloucester, MA	
Sch	*Marion Draper*	stranded	Canal Flats, Vineyard Haven, MA	
Sch	*Mary A. Tyler*	wrecked	North Brewster, Cape Cod, MA	
Sch	*Mary B. Rogers*	stranded	Hough's Neck, Quincy, MA	
Sch	*Mary Cabral*	stranded	Provincetown, MA	
Sch	*Mary E. Cuff*	ashore	Port Jefferson, L.I., NY	
Sch	*Mary Emerson*	stranded	Plymouth, MA	
Slp	*Mattie E.*	wrecked	Lubec, ME	
Sch	*Maynard Sumner*	foundered	off Montauk Point, L.I., NY	
Sch	*Melinda Wood*	wrecked	Hyannis, MA	
Sch	*Mertis H. Perry*	stranded	near Brant Rock, Marshfield, MA	5
Sch	*Meteor*	stranded	Smith's Cove, Gloucester, MA	
Sch	*Michael Henry*		Provincetown, MA	
Sch	*Mildred and Blanch*	stranded	Provincetown, MA	
Slp	*Milo*	stranded	Boston Harbor, MA	
Sch	*Mingue*		Provincetown, MA	
Slp	*Moorland*	stranded	Rocky Neck Cove, Gloucester, MA	
Sch	*Multnomah*		Boston Harbor, MA	
Sch	*Nantasket*	stranded	Nut Island, Boston Harbor, MA	
Sch	*Narcissus*	foundered	off Montauk Point, L.I., NY	
Sch	*Nathan F. Dickson*	foundered	off Fort Trumbull, New London, CT	
Sch	*Nautilus*	stranded	Provincetown Harbor, MA	
Bge	*Navesink*	wrecked	Boston Harbor, MA	
Y	*Nellie*	stranded	Gloucester Harbor, MA	
Slp	*Nellie B.*		Block Island, RI	
Sch	*Nellie Doe*	stranded	Canal Flats, Vineyard Haven, MA	
Bkn	*Nellie M. Slade*	stranded	Vineyard Haven, MA	
Slp	*Neptune*		Portland, ME	
Cat	*Neverbridge*	stranded	Cuttyhunk, MA	
Sch	*Newburg*	ashore	Vineyard Haven, MA	
Sch	*Newell B. Hawes*	stranded	Plum Island, MA	

Bge	*No. 1*	wrecked	off Point Allerton, Hull, MA	
Bge	*No. 4*	wrecked	off Point Allerton, Hull, MA	3
Stp	*Ohio*	stranded	Spectacle Is., Boston Harbor, MA	
Sch	*Olive Leaf*	foundered	Port Jefferson, L.I., NY	
Cat	*Onita*	stranded	Cuttyhunk, MA	
Sch	*Papetta*		Vineyard Haven, MA	
Bge	*Patterson*	foundered	Long Island Sound, NY	
Sch	*Pearl*	ashore	Bass Harbor, ME	
St s	*Pentagoet*	foundered	off Cape Cod, MA	18
Slp	*Percy*		Block Island, RI	
Slp	*Peter*	stranded	Rocky Neck Cove, Gloucester, MA	
Sch	*Phantom*	wrecked	Plymouth Harbor, MA	
Sch	*Phelomina Manter*		Provincetown, MA	
St s	*Pinafore*	wrecked	Isles of Shoals, NH	
Slp	*Plusculum Bonum*	foundered	off Peddock's Is., Boston Harbor, MA	
St p	*Portland*	foundered	off Race Point, Cape Cod, MA	192
Smk	*Prince*	stranded	Provincetown, MA	
Sch	**Queen Esther*	wrecked	off Gay Head, Marthas Vineyard, MA	
Sch	*Queen of the West*	wrecked	Biddeford Pool, ME	
Sch	*Quetay*	stranded	Canal Flats, Vineyard Haven, MA	
Sch	*Rebecca W. Huddell*	stranded	Vineyard Haven, MA	
Sch	*Reganet*	wrecked	off Long Beach Pt., Gardiners Bay, NY	
Cat	*Reliance*		Point of Woods, NY	
Sch	*Reporter*	stranded	Smith's Cove, Gloucester, MA	
Sch	*Rienzi*	stranded	Niles Beach, Gloucester, MA	
Sch	*Ringleader*		Portsmouth, NH	
Slp	*Rival*	foundered	off Battery Whf., Boston Harbor, MA	
Sch	*Robert A. Kinnier*	stranded	Stage House Beach, Boston Harbor, MA	
Sch	*Rondo*	dismasted	Vineyard Haven, MA	
Sch	*Rose Brothers*		Block Island, RI	
Sch	*Rose Cabral*		Boston Harbor, MA	
Sch	*Ruth M. Martin*	stranded	Provincetown Harbor, MA	
Sch	*S.C. Tryon*	stranded	Fort Point Cove, Stockton Springs, ME	
Sch	*S.F. Maker*		Rockland, ME	
Sch	*S.M. Bird*	stranded	Boston Harbor, MA	
Sch	*Saarbruck*	stranded	Milbridge, ME	

Appendix Two

Sch	*Sadie Willcutt*	stranded	Canal Flats, Vineyard Haven, MA	
Sch	*Samuel W. Tilton*	stranded	Hull, MA	
Sch	*Sarah A. Blaisdell*	collision	Hyannis, MA	
Sch	*Sarah C. Wharf*	stranded	Black Rock, Gloucester, MA	
Sch	*School Girl*	stranded	Provincetown, MA	
Bge	*Scranton*	foundered	Long Island Sound, NY	
Slp	*Screamer*	stranded	Pigeon Cove, Rockport, MA	
Cat	*Secret*	stranded	Cuttyhunk, MA	
Sch	*Senator Frye*	stranded	Gloucester, MA	
Sch	*Seraphine*	stranded	Thompson's Is., Boston Harbor, MA	
Sch	*Silver Spray*		Portland, ME	
Cat	*Sport*	capsized	Cuttyhunk, MA	
Slp	*Spray*	foundered	Gloucester, MA	
Slp	*Startle*	wrecked	So. Boston flats, Boston Harbor, MA	1
Cat	*Stranger*		Block Island, RI	
Sch	*Sylvester Whalen*		Provincetown Harbor, MA	
Sch	*Sylvia*		Provincetown Harbor, MA	
Sch	*T.C. Mahoney*		Marblehead, MA	
Sch	*T.W. Cooper*		Portsmouth, NH	
Tug	*Tamaqua*	stranded	Rainsford Island, Boston Harbor, MA	
Sch	*Tay*	dismasted	Vineyard Haven, MA	
Slp	*Thomas B. Reed*		off Provincetown, MA	
Cat	*Three Friends*	stranded	Cuttyhunk, MA	
Slp	*Trumble*	stranded	Pigeon Cove, Rockport, MA	
	Two Sisters		Portsmouth, NH	
Sch	*Two Forty*	stranded	Plymouth Harbor, MA	
Slp	*Union*	stranded	State Wharf, Boston Harbor, MA	
Sch	*Unique*		Cape Cod, MA	
Lch	*Unknown*	stranded	Thompson's Is., Boston Harbor, MA	
Sch	*Unknown*	stranded	Moon Is., Boston Harbor, MA	
Slp	*Unknown*	stranded	Moon Is., Boston Harbor, MA	
Slp	*Unknown*	stranded	Moon Is., Boston Harbor, MA	
	Unknown		Boothbay Harbor, ME	all hands
Sch	*Unknown*	stranded	Black Rock, Cohasset, MA	
Sch	*Unknown*	foundered	inside Hangman's Is., Dorchester Bay, MA	
Sch	*Unknown*		Cape Cod, MA	

Sch	Unknown		Cape Cod, MA	
Sch	Valetta	stranded	Vineyard Haven, MA	
Slp	Valkyrie		Block Island, RI	
Sch	Vamoose	wrecked	Clay Head, Block Island, RI	2
Sch	Venus	stranded	Clark's Island, Plymouth, MA	
Cat	Verena		off Barnstable, MA	
St s	Vigilant	wrecked	Provincetown, MA	
Sch	Virgin Rock		Boston Harbor, MA	
Sch	Virginia	stranded	Thompson's Is., Boston Harbor, MA	2
Bge	Virginia	foundered	off Cohasset, MA	5
Cat	*Vivian	wrecked	off Gay Head, Martha's Vineyard, MA	
Sch	W.H. DeWitt	stranded	Forest River, Salem Harbor, MA	
Sch	W.H.Y. Hackett	stranded	off So. Boston Flats, Boston Harbor, MA	1
Sch	Walker Armington	foundered	Massachusetts Bay	all hands
Sch	Watchman	stranded	Thompson's Is., Boston Harbor, MA	
Slp y	We Are Here	stranded	Stage Island Beach, Boston Harbor, MA	
Bge	Weehauken	stranded	Mystic River, CT	
Sch	White Wings	foundered	Massachusetts Bay	13
Sch	Wild Rose		Cranberry Isles, ME	
Sch	William A. Morse	stranded	Provincetown, MA	
Smk	William Dyer	stranded	Provincetown, MA	
Sch	William Leggett		Rockport, MA	
Smk	Willie		Provincetown, MA	
Sch	Wilson and Willard	stranded	Ten Pound Island, Gloucester, MA	
Sch	Winnie Lawry	stranded	Canal Flats, Vineyard Haven, MA	
Sch	Wm. M. Everett		Long Island, NY	
Sch	Wm. P. Davis	wrecked	near Saunderstown, RI	
Sch	Wm. Todd		Vineyard Haven, MA	
	Woodruff		Northport, ME	
Sch	Young America	stranded	new State Dock, Boston Harbor, MA	

* Gay Head LSS crews altogether rescued 29 persons from the schooners *Queen Esther*, *Vivian*, and *Clara C. Baker*. Seven others perished before help could reach them. It is unknown how many of the seven who were lost belonged to a particular vessel.

Appendix Two

BIBLIOGRAPHY

ARCHIVAL SOURCES

Edward Rowe Snow Archives. Department of Special Collections, Mugar Library, Boston University, Boston, Massachusetts. Boxes 29-31: Documents, correspondence, newspaper clippings, etc. concerning the steamer *Portland* and the gale of November 1898.

Records of the U.S. Coast Guard. Record Group 26, National Archives and Records Administration, Waltham, Massachusetts. *Journals of the U.S. Life-Saving Service* (various stations and dates).

Special Collections of the Maine Historical Society, Portland, Maine. *Eastern Steamship Lines, Inc.—History and Report* (typescript copy by A.M. Austin, Boston, 1924).

BOOKS AND ARTICLES

Annual Report of the Operations of the United States Life-Saving Service, 1899. Washington, D.C.: U.S. Government Printing Office.

List of Merchant Vessels of the United States, 1895-1898. Washington, D.C.: U.S. Government Printing Office.*Monthly Weather Review.* XXVI, No. 11 (November 1898): 493-495.

Berman, Bruce D. *Encyclopedia of American Shipwrecks.* Boston: The Mariners Press, Inc., 1972.

Bradlee, Francis B.C. *Some Account of Steam Navigation in New England.* Salem, MA: The Essex Institute, 1920.

Chase, Virginia. "Shipwreck: the *Portland* Disaster." *DownEast* IV, No. 4 (January 1958): 16-18, 39-40, 42-44.

Dalton, J.W. *The Life Savers of Cape Cod.* Sandwich, MA: J.W. Dalton, 1902.

Eames, Thomas Harrison. "The Wreck of the Steamer *Portland.*" *New England Quarterly* XIII, No. 2 (June 1940): 191-206.

Fish, John Perry. *Unfinished Voyages: A Chronology of Shipwrecks in the Northeastern United States.* Orleans, MA: Lower Cape Publishing, 1989.

Freitas, Fred and Dave Ball. *Warnings Ignored!: The Story of the Portland Gale of 1898.* Scituate, MA: 1995.

Hughes, Patrick. *American Weather Stories.* Washington, D.C.: U.S. Department of Commerce, 1976.

Kittredge, Henry C. *Mooncussers of Cape Cod.* Cambridge, MA: The Riverside Press, 1937.

Ludlum, David. The Country Journal *New England Weather Book.* Boston: Houghton Mifflin Company, 1976.

Pappas, Chrys. "The *Portland* Comes Home." *Portlan Monthly* IV, No. V (July/August 1989): 10-13, 75.

Parsons, Eleanor C. *Thacher's: island of the twin lights.* Canaan, NH: Phoenix Publishing, 1985.

Richardson, John M. *Steamship Lore of the Penobscot: an Informal Story of Steamboating in Maine's Penobscot Region.* Augusta, ME: Kennebec Journal Print Shop, 1941.

Rideout, E.B. "The Day the Weather Bureau Was Right." *Yankee* 20, No. 11 (November 1956):

Seligson, Susan V. "How They Found the *Portland.*" *Yankee* 53, No. 12 (December 1989): 68-75, 120-125.

Small, Isaac M. *Shipwrecks on Cape Cod: the Story of a Few of the Many Hundred Shipwrecks Which Have Occurred on Cape Cod.* Old Greenwich, CT: The Chatham Press, Inc, 1967.

Snow, Edward Rowe. *Great Storms and Famous Shipwrecks of the New England Coast.* Boston: The Yankee Publishing Company, 1943.

———. *New England Sea Tragedies.* New York, Dodd,

Mead & Company, 1960.

———. *Strange Tales from Nova Scotia to Cape Hatteras.* New York: Dodd, Mead & Company, 1949.

———. *The Vengeful Sea.* New York, Dodd, Mead & Company, 1956.

———. *True Tales of Terrible Shipwrecks.* New York: Dodd, Mead & Company, 1963.

Webb, Judge Nathan B. *Opinion of Court and Final Decree in the Matter of the Libel or Petition of the Portland Steamship Company, Owner of the Steamship "Portland" for Limitation of Liability.* Portland, Maine: 1899.

Whitnam, Donald R. *A History of the U.S. Weather Bureau.* Urbana, IL: University of Illinois Press, 1961.

NEWSPAPERS

Boston Daily Advertiser	*New York Times*
Boston Evening Transcript	*Portland* (Maine) *Daily Advertiser*
Boston Globe	*Portland* (Maine) *Evening Express*
Boston Herald	*Portland* (Maine) *Transcript*
Boston Journal	*Provincetown Advocate*
Eastern Daily Argus	*Saturday Globe* (Utica, New York)

The National Observer

PERSONAL INTERVIEWS

Capt. Joseph Roderick, North Truro, Massachusetts

Several conversations with Edward Rowe Snow over the years regarding the loss of the *Portland.* The discussions took place in Portland, Maine at a private lunch with both authors and at Snow's Marshfield, Massachusetts home with one of the authors and at the WNAC radio studio with the other author.

ILLUSTRATION SOURCES

Frontispiece, Collection of The Provincial Press; xii, Fall River Maritime Museum; 2,3,4,5, Blue Hill Meteorological Observatory; 7, Collection of the Cape Cod Pilgrim Memorial Association; 8-9, National Museum of American History, The Smithsonian Institution, Washington, DC; 10, *Portland Evening Express*; 11, Collection of the Cape Cod Pilgrim Memorial Association; 12, Collection of Robert T. Mortimer; 13, Collection of Peter Dow Bachelder; 14, Collection Kenneth E. Thompson, Jr; 15, Maine Maritime Museum, reproduced with the permission of Raymond Prosser, the artist; 17, *Boston Globe*; 18, Steamship Historical Society; 20, Collection of James Elliott; 21, Maine Maritime Museum; 22, *Boston Herald*; 24, *Boston Herald*, both; 25, *Boston Herald*; 26, left, Maine Historical Society, right, Chris C. Church; 27, both, Maine Historical Society; 28, *Boston Herald*; 29, *Boston Herald*; 30, Robert T. Mortimer; 31, *Boston Herald*,; 32, *Boston Herald* 34, *Boston Globe*; 35, Collection William P. Quinn; 36, *Boston Herald*; 37, *Boston Globe*; 39, Greeleys Mill Cartography; 40, 41, *Boston Globe*; 42, 44, Collection of William P. Quinn; 46, 47, 48, 49, 52, *Boston Globe*; 57, *Boston Herald*; 58, Collection of the Cape Cod Pilgrim Memorial Association; 59, *Boston Globe*; 60, *Boston Herald*; 61, Collection William P. Quinn; 62, 63, *Boston Globe*; 64, Collection of Sara Fuller, both; 65, *Boston Herald* and *Boston Globe*; 67, Maine Historical Society; 68, Penobscot Maritime Museum; 71, Collection of Peter Bow Bachelder; 72, Greeleys Mills Cartography; 74, Allie Ryan Collection, 75, Maine Maritime Museum; 76, Maine Maritime Museum; 78, *Boston Herald* and *Boston Globe*; 81, Collection of Mason Philip Smith; 84, Collection of Robert T. Mortimer; 87, Collection Kenneth E. Thompson, Jr.; 88, Collection of the Cape Cod Pilgrim Memorial Association; 89, Collection of Arnold H. Valcour; 90, Collection of Peter Dow Bachelder; 92, Connie Elliott; 93, 94 *Boston Globe*; 96, Collection of William P. Quinn; 97, The Portland Newspapers; 99, 101, Edward Rowe Snow Archive, Special Collections Department, Mugar Library, Boston University; 102, Collection of William P. Quinn; 103, 104, The Portland Newspapers; 105, Edward Rowe Snow; 106, Collection of Arnold H. Valcour; 107, Mason Philip Smith

About The Authors

Peter Dow Bachelder is a Maine native and a graduate of the University of Maine at Orono. Following a period with the U.S. Weather Bureau, he devoted his career to service in Maine's tourism industry and spent 30 years as Director of Information Services at the Maine Publicity Bureau.

Throughout his professional life he has maintained an interest in Maine and its history. Growing up on the coast, he developed an early familiarity with, and a love for the ocean, at the same time developing a yearning to learn more about Maine's unique maritime heritage. For several years he wrote an extensive column about shipwrecks and lighthouses for the *Portland Evening Express*. In addition, he has written two books on these subjects. He is currently writing a comprehensive guide to Bar Harbor and the Downeast region of Maine.

Mason Philip Smith is a Maine native and received his Bachelor of Science degree in Journalism from Boston University's School of Journalism in the College of Communications. He has written a variety of articles about Maine which have appeared in both regional and national publications.

A professional photographer for 30 years, his photographs of Maine, her people and landscape have been exhibited widely and are included in the Permanent Collection of the University of Maine, Orono, and of the Maine Historic Preservation Commission, Augusta. An exhibit of his photographs of the Arkhangelsk region of Russia was held in Russia in 1996.

He is currently working on a book about the German landings in the United States and Canada during World War II.

HUMAROCK SEPARATED FROM MAINLAND
Shingle Beach Disappears

The collections of several New England museums include actual pieces of the steamer *Portland,* or objects washed ashore from the ill-fated vessel. Today, the residents of Scituate and its seacoast village of Humarock have at their doorsteps a living reminder of the damage caused by the Great Gale of 1898.

Prior to the Great Gale, Humarock was a two-mile spit of land connected to the mainland at Scituate by a half-mile of shingle beach. In the center of Humarock a wooden bridge provided additional access to the mainland at Marshfield. A mile further on, at the far end of the sand peninsula, the old entrance of the North and South River system separated Humarock from Marshfield.

At that time, Humarock was a typical beach community. Most of the area was owned by the Fourth Cliff Land Company, which also owned the Hotel Humarock. Near Fourth Cliff there was one house and another building where hunters rented rooms.

In December of 1879 the United States Life-Saving Service established a Life-Saving station at Fourth Cliff. It housed a 25-foot life saving boat and seven surfmen, commanded in 1898 by Captain Frederick Stanley. The station's southern patrol route took the surfmen to the mouth of the North River at what is now Marshfield's Rexhame Beach.

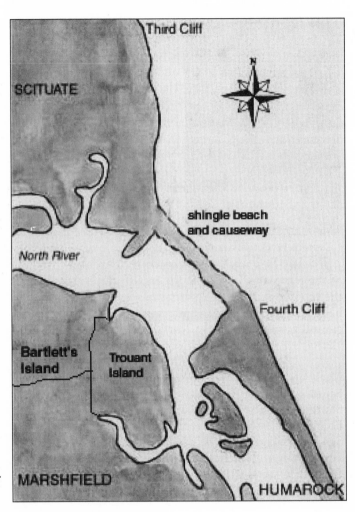

Captain Frederick Stanley
U.S. Life-Saving Service

The northern patrol route found the surfmen striding across the sand causeway and on to Third Cliff and Scituate Harbor.

Richard Wherity, Surfman No. 5, was assigned the northern patrol route the night of November 26th. His watch was to begin at eight p.m. and end at midnight. Wherity, impressed with the rapidly deteriorating weather, decided that the regular patrol across the shingle beach to Third Cliff would have to wait. Because of the increasing danger of the rapidly developing storm, the veteran surfman felt his first mission that night should be to alert unwary duck hunters in the salt-water marshes rimming the edges of the North River behind the Fourth Cliff and the nearby Marshfield mainland.

At the time, at least two hunter's shelters were occupied. Three brothers, William, Everett, and Richard Clapp, of the Scituate village of Greenbush, were at their shanty on the South River near Marshfield's Snake Hill. Up river, behind Fourth Cliff, Fred and Bert Henderson of Norwell, another Scituate village, and their friends Albert Tilden, George Ford, along with George Webster, a young boy, were comfortable in the Henderson's shack.

Surfman Wherity, arriving at the Henderson's location in the station's surfboat, warned the duck hunters that the storm was growing more intense and that they should consider evacuating their refuge. He then returned to the Fourth Cliff Station, taking young George Webster with him.

The Clapps, across the river on the Marshfield shore, received no warning of what was about to transpire. Alarmed by the fierceness of the growing wind and rain, they fled their precarious position in a small duck hunting boat. Almost as soon as they started, towering waves nearly swamped the frail craft. Just as it seemed they would all perish, the trio spied a stray hay-carrying gundalow, which had been torn loose from its mooring. Incredibly, they were able to leap from their sinking craft onto the larger gundalow.

Shaken and oarless, the Clapps found themselves wallowing up to their waists in cold water as the gundalow was swept towards the Marshfield shore, where it eventually

The half-mile shingle beach which connected Humarock with Scituate prior to the Portland Gale. (*Courtesy of Cynthia Krusell*)

grounded. During their frightening passage, they heard anguished cries for help from the Hendersons, who were also trying to make their way to safety in a small skiff. The Clapps were helpless to lend a hand and could only watch and listen as the unforgiving storm carried the Hendersons and their friends to their tragic destiny.

As the storm raged across Scituate and Humarock, hurricane force winds pounded the Fourth Cliff Life-Saving Station, where it tore an out-building from its foundation, ripped the flag pole down, snapped shingles from the main building, and washed a series of platforms away from the front steps.

Whipping across the open expanse of Massachusetts Bay, the huge gale piled up mountainous seas inundating the half-mile sand, stone, and grass causeway linking Humarock to Scituate, gouging a giant break through the shingle beach.

Instantly the gap filled as the Bay and the North River joined, creating an inlet that still exists today. It remains a century-old, living record of the overwhelming ferocity of the Great Gale of 1898.

Venturing outside after the storm's passage, Keeper Frederick Stanley and the other Fourth Cliff Life-Saving Service crews were astounded to find their shingle beach patrol route to Third Cliff had disappeared! The coastline had been permanently altered, making Humarock an island, a situation which remained until the early 1900s, when the old mouth of the North and South river systems silted over, creating a tenuous link to the Marshfield mainland.

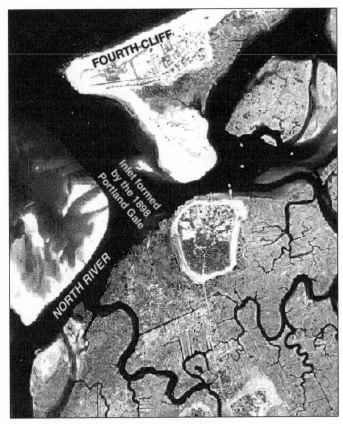

A recent air photo showing the inlet created by the Great Gale of 1898. *(U.S. Coast and Geodetic Survey)*

Appendix Three

FOUR SHORT BLASTS, The Gale of 1898 and The Loss of the Steamer Portland was set in 11 point Adobe Minion. It was printed on 60 lb. Writers Natural acid-free paper by McNaughton & Gunn of Saline, Michigan. The book was designed and published by The Provincial Press of Portland, Maine as a centennial history.